Life in the UK Test
Study Guide

The essential study guide for
the British citizenship test

FOR SALE

WITHDRAWN
FROM STOCK

D1333912

Published by Red Squirrel Publishing

Red Squirrel Publishing

Suite 235, 77 Beak Street,

London W1F 9DB, United Kingdom

www.redsquirrelbooks.com

First edition published in 2006

Tenth Edition – First Impression

Study Guide: 978-1-907389-32-0

Study Guide + CD ROM: 978-1-907389-33-7

Edited by Henry Dillon & George Sandison
Assisted by Gary Budden

Proofreading by Frances King

Picture research by Isaac Strang

Designed and typeset by Cox Design Limited, Witney, Oxon

Printed and bound in the Czech Republic by Finidr

Table of Contents

Introduction

Choosing to become a British citizen is an exciting decision, one made by 131,000 people in 2014. However, the decision to become a British citizen or permanent resident is only the start of what can be a long and challenging journey. The application process is complex, time-consuming and expensive.

An important part of the process is the Life in the UK Test. The Life in the UK Test was revised on 25 March 2013 and this book is based on that 3rd edition of the test. The new test requires you to learn about British history, culture and law based on information provided by the Home Office. This book will make learning this information a whole lot easier.

Home Office statistics show that around three in ten people failed the test in 2014. At £50 for every test taken this is an expensive mistake, and an unnecessary one. Feedback from our customers shows that over 92% pass **first time**.

By using this book to learn the required material, you can walk into your test confident that you will be one of the people who pass the test on their first attempt, and you will be one important step closer to making Britain your home.

Get in touch

We are always delighted when we hear from our readers. If you have any comments or questions about your studies and test, the book or website, or would like to share a particular experience, please get in touch with us.

To send us feedback please visit:
www.lifeintheuk.net/feedback

 Find us on Facebook
www.facebook.com/lifeintheuk.net

 Follow us on Twitter
@lifeintheuk

WHAT'S IN THIS BOOK?

This guide gives you everything you need to prepare for the 3rd revision of the Life in the UK Test. This includes:

- The complete official testable materials, which are chapters 2–6. The material here is exactly the same as given by the Home Office in *Life in the United Kingdom: A guide for new residents*.

- Free access to the online tests at www.lifeintheuk.net.

- Diagrams, illustrations and appendices.

The 3rd edition of the Life in the UK Test contains a lot of dates, events and numbers. We have picked out the most complicated parts and provided illustrations to help you learn them, as well as providing extra appendices to help you study, something which you won't find in the official guide.

How to use this study guide

This guide has many parts and features, but the parts of the book that you must focus on for your test are the official study materials (see chapters 2–6). These study materials have been reproduced in full from the Home Office publication, *Life in the United Kingdom: A guide for new residents*. You must make sure you read and understand these chapters as the questions that you will be asked when you sit your test are based on all of the information provided there.

The testable study materials are divided into five sections:

- The values and principles of the UK

- What is the UK?

- A long and illustrious history

- A modern, thriving society

- The UK government, the law and your role.

Chapter 1 is not testable and includes information on the questions as well as advice from people who passed the test and answers to some of their most common questions.

The other parts of this book support the study materials by making them easier to understand and learn. There are also practice tests that will help you prepare for your test by checking your knowledge.

APPENDICES

This study guide contains timelines that summarise some of the study materials. There is also an extensive glossary of words that you need to know. These are words or phrases that you will need to understand for your test and that you need to know to give you background to the official study materials. Each word or phrase is explained fully, in easy-to-understand language. As you work your way through the materials, you can use the glossary to check any terms or expressions that are not familiar.

PRACTICE QUESTIONS

Once you've finished revising the study materials, try answering the practice questions. This will help you test your knowledge and identify any areas which you need to study further.

Further practice tests, along with news and up-to-date information about the material in this guide can also be found online at **www.lifeintheuk.net**.

REGISTER YOUR BOOK

When you are ready to start taking practice tests, you can use your guide to claim a free subscription to the online tests at www.lifeintheuk.net/test.

Once you have created your account, follow the instructions to get a free 24-hour subscription. You can claim this free subscription as many times as you like.

Get the BritTest app on your iPhone

Take practice tests wherever you go with hundreds of questions and randomised practice tests in your hand.

The essential revision aid for anyone on the move. Available from **www.lifeintheuk.net/app** and the App Store.

You can scan this QR code with your iPhone and go straight to the App Store. If you can't scan it, you can download a free barcode reader app.

CHAPTER 1
About the Test

→ THE LIFE IN THE UK TEST is designed to test your knowledge of British life and ability to use the English language.

The 3rd edition of the citizenship test was launched on 25 March 2013. This guide is for this 3rd version of the citizenship test only.

- Applicants are given 45 minutes to complete the test
- The test is made up of 24 multiple-choice questions
- Questions are chosen at random
- The pass mark is 75% (18 questions correct out of 24)
- Each attempt to pass the test costs £50 (as of October 2015)
- The test is conducted at around 60 Life in the UK Test centres across the UK
- Applicants sit the test using a computer, which is provided by the test centre

Why do I need to take the test?

If you are applying for Indefinite Leave to Remain in the UK (also known as settlement) or British citizenship then as part of your application you must demonstrate that you have sufficient 'knowledge of life and language in the UK'. This is also called the KOL requirement.

You must do two things to meet this requirement:

- pass the Life in the UK Test **AND**
- have a speaking and listening qualification in English at B1 CEFR or higher, or its equivalent.

Some exemptions to the language requirements apply. For instance, if you have a degree-level qualification, or higher, taught in English, you do not have to pass an English language test. You are also exempt if you are from a majority English speaking country, such as the USA or Australia.

What do I need to study?

The Home Office has given some official advice as to what to study. However, the test itself is still very much shrouded in secrecy. The following advice is based on feedback from our readers – people like you who have taken the test – and our personal experience of taking the test. It is intended to help you plan your studies, and not to provide shortcuts!

DO I REALLY NEED TO LEARN EVERYTHING?

The questions in your test 'will be based on the whole book, including [Chapter 2], so make sure you study the entire book thoroughly' (see pages 4–5). This means you may get questions on, for instance, the values and principles of the UK explained in Chapter 2 alongside the information about the test itself.

The questions in your test could be drawn from any part of chapters 2–6. For example, they may be on the Second World War or Parliament today, both of which are covered at length. But you may also be asked about the Statute of Rhuddlan (see page 17) or

British Crown dependencies (see page 8), both of which are only mentioned briefly.

What are the questions like?

The following gives specific advice on the kind of knowledge you must have to pass the test. There are detailed notes on typical question formats at the start of Chapter 8.

> Since the official materials were published in 2013, customers have highlighted places where the official materials are inaccurate.
>
> We have highlighted these points for you in the margins of the text where they arise. These clarifications will not be reflected in the test, and you may be asked questions based on these inaccurate statements. You must learn the text as published by the Home Office.

DATES

The study materials say that 'Questions are based on ALL parts of the handbook, but you will not need to remember dates of birth or death' (see page 4). You must understand, however, when key events happened, or when certain individuals lived. For example, you will not be asked a question such as 'What year was Isaac Newton born in?', though you could be asked 'Which scientist, born in 1643, discovered that white light is made up of the colours of the rainbow?'

ANNUAL EVENTS

One exception with dates is annual events and festivals. Where something happens on the same date each year, such as Christmas or St George's Day, you must know the specific date. These dates are summarised on page 157. For moveable festivals such as Easter or Hannukah, you need to know in which months of the year it normally falls.

FAMOUS PEOPLE, PLACES AND WORKS

You need to be able to correctly identify the famous people described in the text. This means you should know who they are, their nationality and what they are famous for, and be able to name their works. This applies to people described in the text and also people summarised in boxes or lists, including: writers (see page 86), artists (see page 83), films and directors (see page 91), sportspeople (see pages 74–5) and architects (see pages 84–5).

The same is true of famous works or places such as British inventions (see pages 56–7), cities of the UK (see pages 62–3) or the Commonwealth and EU (see pages 123–5). You may be required to correctly identify inventions or inventors, identify British cities or answer a question on who wrote a particular novel, for example.

PERIODS OF HISTORY

Take some time to understand the differences between criminal and civil law, and the kinds of crimes each concerns.

Much of British history is referred to in the context of who was in power at the time. Significant examples are the Elizabethan and Victorian periods. You should think about who was monarch or Prime Minister at the time of key events. For instance, note that King John was on the throne at the time of the Magna Carta, or that Margaret Thatcher was the Prime Minister and leader of the Conservative government when Argentina invaded the Falkland Islands in 1982. The timelines in the appendices at the back of this book (see pages 158–69) highlight the monarch or government in power during different historical periods.

THE UK COURTS

Take some time to understand the differences between criminal and civil law, and the kinds of crimes each concerns (see pages 126–7). You also need to understand which courts deal with certain offences, and how they vary in their processes, in particular the differences between countries in the UK. You should know about Scottish courts even if you are taking the test in London.

You should also take the time to learn some of the more specific details of the criminal and civil courts. For example, the number of members in a jury or the maximum amount that can be claimed in the small claims procedure.

QUESTION STYLES

As well as being required to identify significant dates, you will be tested on your understanding of key people and events. You should expect facts in the test to be presented in a different way to the study materials.

For example, you might be asked 'Is the statement below TRUE or FALSE?' about statements such as 'The hovercraft was invented in the 1950s' or 'Wales united with England during the reign of Henry VIII.' To answer these questions, you need to know that the hovercraft was invented in the 1950s (see page 56) and that Wales was annexed to England during Edward I's reign 300 years before Henry VIII in 1284 (see page 17).

If you learn the materials like a script, you may find certain questions difficult. For example, as well as being asked 'What is Roger Bannister famous for?', you may be asked instead 'Who ran the first four-minute mile in 1954?' Or, instead of 'When were women first given the right to vote?', you may be asked 'Why is 1918 an important date in the history of women's rights?'

You are being tested on your understanding of the subjects covered in the materials rather than how skilled you are at memorising facts.

A question might include dates alongside other facts and ask you which are correct. For example, you might be asked:

Which famous female novelist, born in 1775, wrote novels concerned with marriage and family relationships?

A J K Rowling

B Emily Brontë

C Jane Austen

D Agatha Christie

This question requires you to know that Jane Austen wrote novels that are concerned with marriage and family relationships, but also to be aware of when she was born.

The key is that you should expect to be tested on a whole topic, and not single facts. You can't just learn that Jane Austen wrote *Pride and Prejudice*. You must learn when she lived and what her novels are concerned with.

UNDERSTANDING IS CRUCIAL

The most important thing is to make sure you read and understand all of the materials completely. You should not study this book as a series of isolated facts. Ideally you should be able to explain the contents of the materials in your own words.

You must not ignore anything because it seems too obvious or too general.

You should also try and learn how each fact relates to when it happened.

You can test your understanding on different topics by asking yourself:

- Who was monarch at the time?
- What was the period known as and why?
- What were the causes or outcomes of key events?

For example, you should know about Florence Nightingale and Isambard Kingdom Brunel (see pages 42–3) but also need to think of them as famous Victorians, and people who were alive during the Enlightenment and Industrial Revolution. To give another example, you should know that the Tower of London was built on the orders of William the Conqueror after the Norman Conquest and its White Tower is an example of a Norman castle keep. As well as that, it is home to Beefeaters and the Crown Jewels, and is also the place where Anne Boleyn was executed.

Our appendices are designed to help you develop this kind of understanding. As well as providing a summary of key information they demonstrate the associations you should be making between facts. You should use the appendices to supplement your own studies. If you only study the appendices you will not pass your test.

Do not assume that the test questions will be phrased in the same way as this book, or that you will be asked any of the same questions. You cannot simply learn the practice questions and expect to pass. You must understand the complete study materials.

How to pass your test

STEP 1: STUDY THE MATERIALS

All the questions that can be asked in the Life in the UK Test are based on the official study materials provided by the Home Office. The relevant material has been fully reproduced in this guide.

Your official test will only ask questions based on chapters 2, 3, 4, 5 and 6 of this publication. The questions in this book are also drawn only from those chapters.

Make sure you read the advice from our readers below – this comes from people, just like you, who have already taken the test. Included are specific tips on the kind of thing the test covers, and problems previous customers have faced.

Also remember, **there is no substitute for studying chapters 2–6 thoroughly!**

STEP 2: TAKE PRACTICE TESTS

Once you've finished thoroughly reviewing the study materials you should check if you are ready to take the official test by completing practice tests from this book. It is important to make sure that you fully understand the content and haven't just memorised the information as written, or worse just memorised the questions and answers.

Each of the practice tests contains 24 questions. Each test contains questions covering all parts of the study materials. These questions will not necessarily be phrased in the same way as the text in the chapters.

If you do not pass the practice tests consistently, or do not feel confident enough to sit your official test, then you should continue your study. If you do not have sufficient time left before your official test to do more study, then you may be able to reschedule your test appointment.

Once you've finished with the questions in this book, additional questions can be found in our separate publication *Life in the UK Test: Practice Questions*. You can also go online and access further tests with our free subscription offer. Visit www.lifeintheuk.net/test to redeem this offer.

The practice questions in this book have been designed to help you check you have acquired the knowledge you need to pass the test. Although they are not the same questions that you will receive in your official test, they are in a similar format, use the same approach and test you on the same official material. The practice tests are not a substitute for reading and understanding chapters 2–6.

STEP 3: BOOK YOUR TEST

You must book your test online through the Life in the UK Test booking website. You will need valid photo ID, a debit or credit card and an email address to book. You must pay the test fee when you book.

When you create an account to book your test you must provide information such as your address, nationality, place of birth and age. You must also provide your Home Office reference number if you have one. You will have been issued with this if you have had previous contact with the Home Office (for example, when applying for an extension of stay).

The following types are acceptable forms of photographic ID:

- a Biometric Residence Permit, which is a residence permit that holds your biometric information, facial image and fingerprints – this document must be in date

- a passport from your country of origin – this document may be out of date

- a UK photocard driving licence, full or provisional – this document must be in date

- a European Union Identity Card – this document must be in date

- an Approved Travel Document, which can be a Home Office UK travel document, a Convention Travel Document (CTD), a Certificate of Identity Document (CID) or a Stateless Persons' Document (SPD) – this document must be in date, or

- an Immigration Status Document, endorsed with a UK Residence Permit and bearing a photo of the holder – this document may be out of date.

It is very important to make sure that the details you register when booking **exactly** match the ID and supporting documents you take with you on the day. If they do not match – for instance, you registered your full middle name but your ID only shows an initial – you will not be allowed to take the test and your test fee will not be refunded. **We have had lots of reports from candidates who have been turned away at the test centre because of this.**

If you have registered for the test with your married name and your ID is in your maiden name, then you must bring an original UK marriage certificate, or a UK Spouse Visa (this must be in date), or a UK Deed Poll (this must show a red seal) to support this. Without one of these your test will be refused and you will not receive a refund.

You must also make sure you bring a valid proof of address no older than three months before your test date. This must be an original version – **no photocopies** – of one of the documents listed on the Life in the UK Test booking website. Valid examples are a bank statement, council tax bill or gas/electricity/water bill, but not a mobile phone bill.

Tests are carried out at around 60 test centres throughout the UK and you will be directed to the five test centres closest to you when you book. You must take your test at one of these five centres. If you book your test elsewhere you will not be allowed to take the test and your fee will not be refunded.

You may have to wait a few weeks for your test appointment. The earliest you can take your test is seven days after booking. You can cancel your test without charge up to seven days before your test. If you cancel within seven days your test fee will not be refunded. You will have to book and pay again. You can change your test appointment using your online account.

You can also call the Life in the UK Test Helpline on 0800 015 4245 with any queries about the booking process.

STEP 4: TAKE AND PASS YOUR TEST

Firstly, it is important to make sure that you have a good night's sleep before the test and that you have eaten beforehand. It may surprise you, but being tired or hungry can severely affect your concentration and make the test harder.

Be sure to arrive earlier than your appointed test time as you will need time to be registered by the test centre staff. If you arrive a few minutes before your test is due to start you may not be allowed to take your test. If this happens you will have to rebook and pay again.

When you arrive at the test centre you will need to register your details and sign a document to confirm your attendance. The registration process before the test itself could take some time as there may be many candidates to register.

You will take the test using a computer provided by the test centre. You will be allowed to run through a few practice questions so that you are familiar with the test software. Some applicants worry that they do not know the answers for the practice questions. However, these questions do not count towards your end result.

Make sure you listen carefully when the test supervisor explains how to use the test software. It is important that you know how to use it. If you are unsure then ask the test supervisor for help. As each applicant's test is begun individually by the test supervisor, your test will not begin until you say that you are ready.

Once your test begins you will have 45 minutes to complete it. You will be able to review and change the answers to your questions at any stage during the test.

If you pass then you will be given a Pass Notification Letter, which you should sign before you leave the test centre. This is an important document and must be attached to your settlement or citizenship application.

You will not be able to get a replacement Pass Notification Letter if you lose it. Make sure you keep it in a safe place.

If you don't pass then you can take the test again. However, you will need to book and pay for another appointment. You must wait at least seven days before retaking your test. You should not make an application for naturalisation as a British citizen or for Indefinite Leave to Remain if you fail. You may need to apply for further leave to remain if your existing leave to remain has expired, or is close to expiring.

Advice from our readers

Our readers often contact us to share their advice and experiences of taking the test. This section is a summary of the most common and insightful comments that we have received.

> *I was told that this study guide was the wrong one*

Staff at some test centres may tell you that you have been using the wrong book to study – this is not true. Whilst the government's own study guides are the official version, there are other independent guides that offer exactly the same material but also provide additional advice that the official guide does not. The only thing you need to check is that the book you are using includes the complete testable materials of the 3rd revised materials, *Life in the United Kingdom: A guide for new residents*, and has been published by a reputable publisher.

> *I wasn't allowed to take my test because I didn't register my middle name*

When you book for your test it is essential that you provide completely accurate information. You must ensure that your name, and other details you provide match exactly the ID you take with you. This means you must provide the information exactly as it appears on your ID. If there is any uncertainty you should contact the helpline before booking. You should also make sure your proof of address is valid and no more than three months old.

> *The test was supposed to start at 1pm but it actually started almost one hour later*

While the test itself lasts 45 minutes, the whole process of the test can last much longer. Some candidates at busy test centres have reported the process from arriving to getting your results taking up to two and a half hours. You should bear this in mind if you are driving to the test and need to park, or have other commitments on the day.

> *I thought I'd get a breakdown of my results*

At the end of the test you will only be told whether you passed or failed. You will not be told your score or what you got wrong. If you fail, you will only be told which sections you answered questions on incorrectly.

> *The official questions were worded differently to the online test questions*

It is very likely that you will not have seen the exact questions that are in the test before. The practice tests are intended to help you prepare and get used to the style of questions of the real test. It is very important that you read every question carefully and that you understand it before you answer.

> *Some questions were difficult to understand. The way it was phrased made it hard to decide what the correct answer was*

It is vital that you read every question thoroughly, and do not make any assumptions about what it is asking you. Think about each option and how it relates to the question carefully. However difficult a question is remember that, if you have read all the chapters in the book, you will have seen the answer before.

> *It would be helpful if they had a translation of the test and the book in my language*

The test serves two purposes: it tests your understanding of the study materials and it tests that you can read and understand English. If you cannot read English well then you are unlikely to pass the test.

> *I failed because I relied on the practice tests and did not study the chapters in any detail*

Just taking practice tests is not sufficient preparation. Questions in your test can be taken from every part of chapters 2, 3, 4, 5 and 6 of this book. You will not understand all of the material you may be tested on just by taking practice tests. In addition to taking practice tests, you must read the study materials thoroughly.

> *I did not feel comfortable asking the test centre staff for help*

The test supervisors are there to help you. If you are unsure of anything then you must ask. They will assist you if you have any problems with your computer or if you are uncomfortable in any way, but they will not help you with the answers!

> *I didn't realise 30 of us would take the test at the same time*

You will not be taking the test alone. You will be taking the test with a number of other people who have booked the same time at your test centre. You will be asked questions by the test centre staff, but it is not the same as an interview at a visa application centre. You will be given your own computer and your own space.

> *My daughter and husband were not allowed to wait for me in the building. We should have been told about this before the test*

The government's test booking platform says 'You can't bring children or other family members with you to the centre'. It is best to assume your family will not be able to wait for you in the test centre. If you intend to be accompanied by friends or family members we suggest you call the test centre in advance to see if there is somewhere nearby where they can wait for you.

Your application – common problems

A small percentage of citizenship applications are refused. In 2014, over 5,700 applications (5%) were refused. The top six reasons for these refusals were as follows:

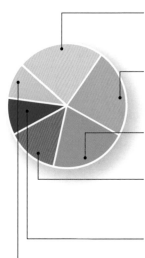

Delays in responding to queries from the UK Border Agency: 21.6%
• Additional information not supplied when requested
• Unable to contact applicant

Residency requirements not satisfied: 21.4%
• Are not living lawfully in the UK
• Have been outside the UK for more than 90 days in a 12-month period

Applicant not of good character: 19.2%
• Recurring criminal history or unspent conviction
• Considered a threat to national security

Application not correctly completed: 12.75%
• Late and improper applications
• Application fee not paid
• Unacceptable documentation submitted

Parent not a British citizen: 8.9%

Insufficient knowledge of life or language in the UK: 8.6%
• Insufficient or incorrect English language qualifications
• No pass certificate for the Life in the UK Test

Six people were refused because they didn't attend their citizenship ceremony in time. Don't let that happen to you!

You should not send your application more than 28 days before you become eligible to apply. If you do, the Home Office may refuse your application on grounds of the residency requirements not being satisfied and they will not refund any fees paid. However, you must ensure you make your application before your current permission to stay in the UK expires.

APPLICATION CHECKING SERVICES

If you want to check that your Indefinite Leave to Remain or citizenship application is complete you can use the Settlement and

Nationality Checking Services offered by most local authorities. These services have two main advantages:

1 Your application, along with all supporting documentation, will be checked and completed correctly before being sent, ensuring it is processed promptly.

2 Certified copies are taken of valuable supporting documents – such as passports – allowing you to keep the originals.

A directory of councils offering these services can be found on our website, www.lifeintheuk.net/ncs and www.lifeintheuk.net/scs. There is a fee payable for this service – the amount depends on your local council. This service is very popular, so make sure you contact them before you want to send your application to ensure you get an appointment.

Share your experiences

We are able to give you advice like this because of the hugely helpful feedback we have had from our readers. We read everything people write to us and use it all when we make new editions of this book every year.

The more feedback we get the better we can make this advice. So we want to hear about your experiences of the test. In particular, we want to hear what you think we did well or what we didn't do so well. Was there a particular type of question you weren't expecting? Did one of our study aids really help you?

Everything from a single thought to a detailed critique of every question in your test is useful. To send us feedback just visit www.lifeintheuk.net/feedback.

Test Preparation Checklist

There are a lot of things that you need to remember to do for the Life in the UK Test. Avoid problems and get organised by completing this checklist.

◯ **Test appointment booked**

Book your test through the Life in the UK Test booking website

Test Date

Time

Test Centre Address

Phone

◯ **Finished reading study materials (see chapters 2–6)**

◯ **Completed all practice tests in study guide**

◯ **Completed free online practice tests at www.lifeintheuk.net**

◯ **Checked latest tips and advice at www.lifeintheuk.net**

◯ **Checked your registered details exactly match your photo ID**

◯ **Checked your proof of address is valid and in date**

◯ **Confirmed test centre location and travel route**

CHAPTER 2
The values and principles of the UK

➔ IN THIS CHAPTER you will learn about the fundamental rights and responsibilities which apply to everyone who lives in the UK, citizen or not. There is also some information about the format of the Life in the UK Test and the requirements for becoming a permanent resident.

The questions you get in the real test will be based on the whole book, including this introductory chapter, so make sure that you are familiar with the details of the application process for permanent residence as well as the rights and responsibilities of UK residents.

IN THIS CHAPTER THERE IS INFORMATION ABOUT:

- The fundamental principles of British life
- Responsibilities and freedoms of all UK residents
- Becoming a permanent resident
- Taking the Life in the UK Test
- The testable sections of this book

Britain is a fantastic place to live: a modern, thriving society with a long and illustrious history. Our people have been at the heart of the world's political, scientific, industrial and cultural development. We are proud of our record of welcoming new migrants who will add to the diversity and dynamism of our national life.

Applying to become a permanent resident or citizen of the UK is an important decision and commitment. You will be agreeing to accept the responsibilities which go with permanent residence and to respect the laws, values and traditions of the UK. Good citizens are an asset to the UK. We welcome those seeking to make a positive contribution to our society.

Passing the Life in the UK Test is part of demonstrating that you are ready to become a permanent migrant to the UK. This handbook is designed to support you in your preparation. It will help you to integrate into society and play a full role in your local community. It will also help ensure that you have a broad general knowledge of the culture, laws and history of the UK.

British society is founded on fundamental values and principles which all those living in the UK should respect and support.

The values and principles of the UK

British society is founded on fundamental values and principles which all those living in the UK should respect and support. These values are reflected in the responsibilities, rights and privileges of being a British citizen or permanent resident of the UK. They are based on history and traditions and are protected by law, customs and expectations. There is no place in British society for extremism or intolerance.

The fundamental principles of British life include:

• democracy
• the rule of law
• individual liberty
• tolerance of those with different faiths and beliefs
• participation in community life.

As part of the citizenship ceremony, new citizens pledge to uphold these values. The pledge is:

'I will give my loyalty to the United Kingdom and respect its rights and freedoms. I will uphold its democratic values. I will observe its laws faithfully and fulfil my duties and obligations as a British citizen.'

Flowing from the fundamental principles are responsibilities and freedoms which are shared by all those living in the UK and which we expect all residents to respect.

If you wish to be a permanent resident or citizen of the UK, you should:

• respect and obey the law
• respect the rights of others, including their right to their own opinions
• treat others with fairness
• look after yourself and your family
• look after the area in which you live and the environment.

In return, the UK offers:

• freedom of belief and religion
• freedom of speech
• freedom from unfair discrimination
• a right to a fair trial
• a right to join in the election of a government.

Becoming a permanent resident

To apply to become a permanent resident or naturalised citizen of the UK, you will need to:

• speak and read English
• have a good understanding of life in the UK.

This means you will need to:

• Pass the Life in the UK Test

AND

• Produce acceptable evidence of speaking and listening skills in English at B1 of the Common European Framework of Reference. This is equivalent to ESOL Entry Level 3. There is a wide range of qualifications or ways that may be used to demonstrate this. Some of these test speaking and listening skills only. Others also test reading and writing skills. You will be able to choose a qualification that suits your requirements. For further details on how to demonstrate evidence of the required level of speaking and listening skills in English, please visit the Home Office website.

" Questions are based on ALL parts of the handbook. **"**

It is possible that the requirements may change in the future. You should check the information on the Home Office website for current requirements before applying for settlement or citizenship.

Taking the Life in the UK Test

This handbook will help prepare you for taking the Life in the UK Test. The test consists of 24 questions about important aspects of life in the UK. Questions are based on ALL parts of the handbook, but you will not need to remember dates of birth or death. The 24 questions will be different for each person taking the test at that test session.

The Life in the UK Test is usually taken in English, although special arrangements can be made if you wish to take it in Welsh or Scottish Gaelic.

The Life in the UK Test booking site is now www.gov.uk/ life-in-the-uk-test

You can only take the test at a registered and approved Life in the UK Test centre. There are about 60 test centres around the UK. You can only book your test online, at www.lifeintheuktest.gov.uk. You should not take your test at any other establishment as the Home Office will only accept certificates from registered test centres. If you live on the Isle of Man or in the Channel Islands, there are different arrangements for taking the Life in the UK Test.

When booking your test, read the instructions carefully. Make sure you enter your details correctly. You will need to take some identification and proof of your address with you to the test. If you don't take these, you will not be able to take the test.

HOW TO USE THIS HANDBOOK

Everything that you will need to know to pass the Life in the UK Test is included in this handbook. The questions will be based on the whole book, including this introduction, so make sure you study the entire book thoroughly. The handbook has been written to ensure that anyone who can read English at ESOL Entry Level 3 or above should have no difficulty with the language.

The glossary at the back of the handbook contains some key words and phrases, which you might find helpful.

The 'Check that you understand' boxes are for guidance. They will help you to identify particular things that you should understand. Just knowing the things highlighted in these boxes will not be enough to pass the test. You need to make sure that you understand everything in the book, so please read the information carefully.

> The glossary at the back of the handbook contains some key words and phrases, which you might find helpful.

WHERE TO FIND MORE INFORMATION

You can find out more information from the following places:

- the Home Office website for information about the application process and the forms you will need to complete

- the Life in the UK Test website (www.lifeintheuktest.gov.uk) for information about the test and how to book a place to take one

- gov.uk (www.gov.uk) for information about ESOL courses and how to find one in your area.

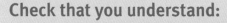

Check that you understand:

- The origin of the values underlying British society
- The fundamental principles of British life
- The responsibilities and freedoms which come with permanent residence
- The process of becoming a permanent resident or citizen

CHAPTER 3
What is the UK?

→ **IN THIS CHAPTER** you will learn about the countries that make up the Union as well as the various phrases used to describe them. Although this chapter is very short you should make sure that you read and understand all the facts presented. For instance it is very likely there will be questions about the differences between Great Britain, the British Isles and Britain, or what the Crown dependencies are.

IN THIS CHAPTER THERE IS INFORMATION ABOUT:

• The different countries that make up the UK

What is the UK?

The UK is made up of England, Scotland, Wales and Northern Ireland. The rest of Ireland is an independent country.

The official name of the country is the United Kingdom of Great Britain and Northern Ireland. 'Great Britain' refers only to England, Scotland and Wales, not to Northern Ireland. The words 'Britain', 'British Isles' or 'British', however, are used in this book to refer to everyone in the UK.

'Great Britain' refers only to England, Scotland and Wales, not to Northern Ireland.

There are also several islands which are closely linked with the UK but are not part of it: the Channel Islands and the Isle of Man. These have their own governments and are called 'Crown dependencies'. There are also several British overseas territories in other parts of the world, such as St Helena and the Falkland Islands. They are also linked to the UK but are not a part of it.

The UK is governed by the Parliament sitting in Westminster. Scotland, Wales and Northern Ireland also have parliaments or assemblies of their own, with devolved powers in defined areas.

Check that you understand:

- The different countries that make up the UK

CHAPTER 4
A long and illustrious history

→ IN THIS CHAPTER you will learn about British history starting from the Stone Age. The beginning focuses on arriving populations which affected the language and religions of Britain. After that the focus is on the development of the monarchy, church and Parliament. Major battles and significant periods are covered, including the civil war, the industrial revolution and the Empire. There is a lot of information about WWI and WWII and after WWII the chapter focuses on the governments of the UK and devolution in Northern Ireland, Wales and Scotland.

Make sure that you understand the relationship between the monarchy and Parliament, Protestants and Catholics and Britain and the colonies of the Empire. Think about how the right to vote developed. You should also make sure you know about each of the people described. You will need to know about the Acts of Parliament and other major events.

IN THIS CHAPTER THERE IS INFORMATION ABOUT:

- The history of early Britain
- The medieval period
- The Tudor and Stuart monarchs of the UK
- The establishment of Parliament

- The unification of the United Kingdom
- The Enlightenment and Industrial Revolution
- The Victorian Age and the British Empire
- The First World War
- The Great Depression

- The Second World War
- Britain since 1945 and the welfare state
- Great British inventions and sporting figures
- Government since the Second World War

Early Britain

The first people to live in Britain were hunter-gatherers, in what we call the Stone Age. For much of the Stone Age, Britain was connected to the continent by a land bridge. People came and went, following the herds of deer and horses which they hunted. Britain only became permanently separated from the continent by the Channel about 10,000 years ago.

The first farmers arrived in Britain about 6,000 years ago. The ancestors of these first farmers probably came from south-east Europe. These people built houses, tombs and monuments on the land. One of these monuments, Stonehenge, still stands in what is now the English county of Wiltshire. Stonehenge was probably a special gathering place for seasonal ceremonies. Other Stone Age sites have also survived. Skara Brae on Orkney, off the north coast of Scotland, is the best preserved prehistoric village in northern Europe, and has helped archaeologists to understand more about how people lived near the end of the Stone Age.

The World Heritage Site of Stonehenge

Around 4,000 years ago, people learned to make bronze. We call this period the Bronze Age. People lived in roundhouses and buried their dead in tombs called round barrows. The people of the Bronze Age were accomplished metalworkers who made many beautiful objects in bronze and gold, including tools, ornaments and weapons. The Bronze Age was followed by the Iron Age, when people learned how to make weapons and tools out of iron. People still lived in roundhouses, grouped together into larger settlements, and sometimes defended sites called hill forts. A very impressive hill fort can still be seen today at Maiden Castle, in the English county of Dorset. Most people were farmers, craft workers or warriors. The language they spoke was part of the Celtic language family. Similar languages were spoken across Europe in the Iron Age, and related languages are still spoken today in some parts of Wales, Scotland and Ireland. The people of the Iron Age had a sophisticated culture and economy. They made the first coins to be minted in Britain, some inscribed with the names of Iron Age kings. This marks the beginnings of British history.

THE ROMANS

Julius Caesar led a Roman invasion of Britain in 55 BC. This was unsuccessful and for nearly 100 years Britain remained separate from the Roman Empire. In AD 43 the Emperor Claudius led the Roman army in a new invasion. This time, there was resistance from some of the British tribes but the Romans were successful in occupying almost all of Britain. One of the tribal leaders who fought against the Romans was Boudicca, the queen of the Iceni in what is now eastern England. She is still remembered today and there is a statue of her on Westminster Bridge in London, near the Houses of Parliament.

Areas of what is now Scotland were never conquered by the Romans, and the Emperor Hadrian built a wall in the north of England to keep out the Picts (ancestors of the Scottish people). Included in the wall were a number of forts. Parts of Hadrian's Wall, including the forts of Housesteads and Vindolanda, can still be seen. It is a popular area for walkers and is a UNESCO (United Nations Education, Scientific and Cultural Organization) World Heritage Site.

The Romans remained in Britain for 400 years. They built roads and public buildings, created a structure of law, and introduced new plants and animals. It was during the 3rd and 4th centuries AD that the first Christian communities began to appear in Britain.

THE ANGLO-SAXONS

The Roman army left Britain in AD 410 to defend other parts of the Roman Empire and never returned. Britain was again invaded by tribes from northern Europe: the Jutes, the Angles and the Saxons. The languages they spoke are the basis of modern-day

One of the tribal leaders who fought against the Romans was Boudicca, the queen of the Iceni in what is now eastern England.

English. Battles were fought against these invaders but, by about AD 600, Anglo-Saxon kingdoms were established in Britain. These kingdoms were mainly in what is now England. The burial place of one of the kings was at Sutton Hoo in modern Suffolk. This king was buried with treasure and armour, all placed in a ship which was then covered by a mound of earth. Parts of the west of Britain, including much of what is now Wales, and Scotland, remained free of Anglo-Saxon rule.

An Anglo-Saxon helmet found at Sutton Hoo – currently on display at the British Museum

The helmet shown in this image is actually a 7th-century Viking helmet that was discovered in Vendel, Sweden, not Sutton Hoo. However, for the purposes of your test you must learn the material as reproduced here.

The Anglo-Saxons were not Christians when they first came to Britain but, during this period, missionaries came to Britain to preach about Christianity. Missionaries from Ireland spread the religion in the north. The most famous of these were St Patrick, who would become the patron saint of Ireland (see pages 67–8 for more about patron saints), and St Columba, who founded a monastery on the island of Iona, off the coast of what is now Scotland. St Augustine led missionaries from Rome, who spread Christianity in the south. St Augustine became the first Archbishop of Canterbury (see page 67 for more about the Archbishop of Canterbury and the Church in Britain today).

THE VIKINGS

The Vikings came from Denmark and Norway. They first visited Britain in AD 789 to raid coastal towns and take away goods and slaves. Then, they began to stay and form their own communities in the east of England and Scotland. The Anglo-Saxon kingdoms in England united under King Alfred the Great, who defeated the Vikings. Many of the Viking invaders stayed in Britain – especially in the east and north of England, in an area known as the Danelaw (many place names there, such as Grimsby and Scunthorpe, come from the Viking languages). The Viking settlers mixed with local communities and some converted to Christianity.

The Anglo-Saxon kingdoms in England united under King Alfred the Great, who defeated the Vikings.

Anglo-Saxon kings continued to rule what is now England, except for a short period when there were Danish kings. The first of these was Cnut, also called Canute.

In the north, the threat of attack by Vikings had encouraged the people to unite under one king, Kenneth MacAlpin. The term Scotland began to be used to describe that country.

THE NORMAN CONQUEST

In 1066, an invasion led by William, the Duke of Normandy (in what is now northern France), defeated Harold, the Saxon king of England, at the Battle of Hastings. Harold was killed in the battle. William became king of England and is known as William the Conqueror. The battle is commemorated in a great piece of embroidery, known as the Bayeux Tapestry, which can still be seen in France today.

Marcel Douwe Dekker

Part of the Bayeux Tapestry – the linen cloth is nearly 70 metres (230 feet) long and is embroidered with coloured wool

The Norman Conquest was the last successful foreign invasion of England and led to many changes in government and social structures in England. Norman French, the language of the new ruling class, influenced the development of the English language as we know it today. Initially the Normans also conquered Wales, but the Welsh gradually won territory back. The Scots and the Normans fought on the border between England and Scotland; the Normans took over some land on the border but did not invade Scotland.

William sent people all over England to draw up lists of all the towns and villages. The people who lived there, who owned the land and what animals they owned were also listed. This was called the Domesday Book. It still exists today and gives a picture of society in England just after the Norman Conquest.

Check that you understand:

• The history of the UK before the Romans

• The impact of the Romans on British society

• The different groups that invaded after the Romans

• The importance of the Norman invasion in 1066

The Middle Ages

WAR AT HOME AND ABROAD

The period after the Norman Conquest up until about 1485 is called the Middle Ages (or the medieval period). It was a time of almost constant war.

The English kings fought with the Welsh, Scottish and Irish noblemen for control of their lands. In Wales, the English were able to establish their rule. In 1284 King Edward I of England introduced the Statute of Rhuddlan, which annexed Wales to the Crown of England. Huge castles, including Conwy and Caernarvon, were built to maintain this power. By the middle of the 15th century the last Welsh rebellions had been defeated. English laws and the English language were introduced.

In Scotland, the English kings were less successful. In 1314 the Scottish, led by Robert the Bruce, defeated the English at the Battle of Bannockburn, and Scotland remained unconquered by the English.

At the beginning of the Middle Ages, Ireland was an independent country. The English first went to Ireland as troops to help the Irish king and remained to build their own settlements. By 1200, the English ruled an area of Ireland known as the Pale, around Dublin. Some of the important lords in other parts of Ireland accepted the authority of the English king.

During the Middle Ages, the English kings also fought a number of wars abroad. Many knights took part in the Crusades, in which European Christians fought for control of the Holy Land. English kings also fought a long war with France, called the Hundred Years War (even though it actually lasted 116 years). One of the most famous battles of the Hundred Years War was the Battle of Agincourt in 1415, where King Henry V's vastly outnumbered English army defeated the French. The English left France in the 1450s.

> **"**
> In 1314 the Scottish, led by Robert the Bruce, defeated the English at the Battle of Bannockburn.
> **"**

THE BLACK DEATH

The Normans used a system of land ownership known as feudalism. The king gave land to his lords in return for help in war. Landowners had to send certain numbers of men to serve in the army. Some peasants had their own land but most were serfs.

They had a small area of their lord's land where they could grow food. In return, they had to work for their lord and could not move away. The same system developed in southern Scotland. In the north of Scotland and Ireland, land was owned by members of the 'clans' (prominent families).

In 1348, a disease, probably a form of plague, came to Britain. This was known as the Black Death. One third of the population of England died and a similar proportion in Scotland and Wales. This was one of the worst disasters ever to strike Britain. Following the Black Death, the smaller population meant there was less need to grow cereal crops. There were labour shortages and peasants began to demand higher wages. New social classes appeared, including owners of large areas of land (later called the gentry), and people left the countryside to live in the towns. In the towns, growing wealth led to the development of a strong middle class.

In Ireland, the Black Death killed many in the Pale and, for a time, the area controlled by the English became smaller.

LEGAL AND POLITICAL CHANGES

In the Middle Ages, Parliament began to develop into the institution it is today. Its origins can be traced to the king's council of advisers, which included important noblemen and the leaders of the Church.

There were few formal limits to the king's power until 1215. In that year, King John was forced by his noblemen to agree to a number of demands. The result was a charter of rights called the Magna Carta (which means the Great Charter). The Magna Carta established the idea that even the king was subject to the law. It protected the rights of the nobility and restricted the king's power to collect taxes or to make or change laws. In future, the king would need to involve his noblemen in decisions.

In England, parliaments were called for the king to consult his nobles, particularly when the king needed to raise money. The numbers attending Parliament increased and two separate parts, known as Houses, were established. The nobility, great landowners and bishops sat in the House of Lords. Knights, who were usually smaller landowners, and wealthy people from towns and cities were elected to sit in the House of Commons. Only a small part of the population was able to join in electing the members of the Commons.

> The Magna Carta established the idea that even the king was subject to the law. It protected the rights of the nobility and restricted the king's power to collect taxes or to make or change laws.

A similar Parliament developed in Scotland. It had three Houses, called Estates: the lords, the commons and the clergy.

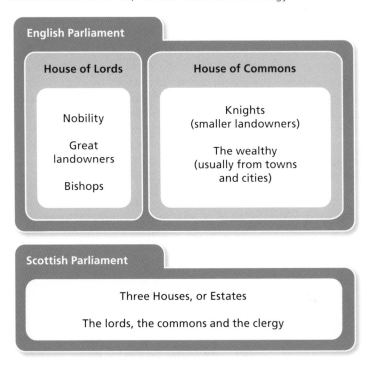

English Parliament

House of Lords

Nobility

Great landowners

Bishops

House of Commons

Knights (smaller landowners)

The wealthy (usually from towns and cities)

Scottish Parliament

Three Houses, or Estates

The lords, the commons and the clergy

This was also a time of development in the legal system. The principle that judges are independent of the government began to be established. In England, judges developed 'common law' by a process of precedence (that is, following previous decisions) and tradition. In Scotland, the legal system developed slightly differently and laws were 'codified' (that is, written down).

A DISTINCT IDENTITY

The Middle Ages saw the development of a national culture and identity. After the Norman Conquest, the king and his noblemen had spoken Norman French and the peasants had continued to speak Anglo-Saxon. Gradually these two languages combined to become one English language. Some words in modern English – for example, 'park' and 'beauty' – are based on Norman French words. Others – for example, 'apple', 'cow' and 'summer' – are based on Anglo-Saxon words. In modern English there are often two words with very similar meanings, one from French and one

> By 1400, in England, official documents were being written in English, and English had become the preferred language of the royal court and Parliament.

from Anglo-Saxon. 'Demand' (French) and 'ask' (Anglo-Saxon) are examples. By 1400, in England, official documents were being written in English, and English had become the preferred language of the royal court and Parliament.

In the years leading up to 1400, Geoffrey Chaucer wrote a series of poems in English about a group of people going to Canterbury on a pilgrimage. The people decided to tell each other stories on the journey, and the poems describe the travellers and some of the stories they told. This collection of poems is called *The Canterbury Tales*. It was one of the first books to be printed by William Caxton, the first person in England to print books using a printing press. Many of the stories are still popular. Some have been made into plays and television programmes.

In Scotland, many people continued to speak Gaelic and the Scots language also developed. A number of poets began to write in the Scots language. One example is John Barbour, who wrote *The Bruce* about the Battle of Bannockburn.

York Minster stained glass

The Middle Ages also saw a change in the type of buildings in Britain. Castles were built in many places in Britain and Ireland, partly for defence. Today many are in ruins, although some, such as Windsor and Edinburgh, are still in use. Great cathedrals – for example, Lincoln Cathedral – were also built, and many of these are still used for worship. Several of the cathedrals had windows of stained glass, telling stories about the Bible and Christian saints. The glass in York Minster is a famous example.

During this period, England was an important trading nation. English wool became a very important export. People came to England from abroad to trade and also to work. Many had special skills, such as weavers from France, engineers from Germany, glass manufacturers from Italy and canal builders from Holland.

THE WARS OF THE ROSES

In 1455, a civil war was begun to decide who should be king of England. It was fought between the supporters of two families: the House of Lancaster and the House of York. This war was called the Wars of the Roses, because the symbol of Lancaster was a red rose and the symbol of York was a white rose. The war ended with the Battle of Bosworth Field in 1485. King Richard III of the House of York was killed in the battle and Henry Tudor, the leader of the House of Lancaster, became King Henry VII. Henry then married King Richard's niece, Elizabeth of York, and united the two families. Henry was the first king of the House of Tudor. The symbol of the House of Tudor was a red rose with a white rose inside it as a sign that the Houses of York and Lancaster were now allies.

| The red rose of Lancaster | The white rose of York | The red and white rose of the House of Tudor |

Check that you understand:

- The wars that took place in the Middle Ages
- How Parliament began to develop
- The way that land ownership worked
- The effect of the Black Death
- The development of English language and culture
- The Wars of the Roses and the founding of the House of Tudor

The Tudors and Stuarts

RELIGIOUS CONFLICTS

After his victory in the Wars of the Roses, Henry VII wanted to make sure that England remained peaceful and that his position as king was secure. He deliberately strengthened the central administration of England and reduced the power of the nobles. He was thrifty and built up the monarchy's financial reserves. When he died, his son Henry VIII continued the policy of centralising power.

Henry VIII was most famous for breaking away from the Church of Rome and marrying six times.

Henry VIII was king of England from 21 April 1509 until his death on 28 January 1547

THE SIX WIVES OF HENRY VIII

Catherine of Aragon – Catherine was a Spanish princess. She and Henry had a number of children but only one, Mary, survived. When Catherine was too old to give him another child, Henry decided to divorce her, hoping that another wife would give him a son to be his heir.

Anne Boleyn – Anne Boleyn was English. She and Henry had one daughter, Elizabeth. Anne was unpopular in the country and was accused of taking lovers. She was executed at the Tower of London.

Jane Seymour – Henry married Jane after Anne's execution. She gave Henry the son he wanted, Edward, but she died shortly after the birth.

Anne of Cleves – Anne was a German princess. Henry married her for political reasons but divorced her soon after.

Catherine Howard – Catherine was a cousin of Anne Boleyn. She was also accused of taking lovers and executed.

Catherine Parr – Catherine was a widow who married Henry late in his life. She survived him and married again but died soon after.

You may be asked specific questions about Henry VIII's wives. As well as the facts given here, you should learn the order he married them in.

To divorce his first wife, Henry needed the approval of the Pope. When the Pope refused, Henry established the Church of England. In this new Church, the king, not the Pope, would have the power to appoint bishops and order how people should worship.

To divorce his first wife, Henry needed the approval of the Pope. When the Pope refused, Henry established the Church of England.

At the same time the Reformation was happening across Europe. This was a movement against the authority of the Pope and the ideas and practices of the Roman Catholic Church. The Protestants formed their own churches. They read the Bible in their own languages instead of in Latin; they did not pray to saints or at shrines; and they believed that a person's own relationship with God was more important than submitting to the authority of the Church. Protestant ideas gradually gained strength in England, Wales and Scotland during the 16th century.

In Ireland, however, attempts by the English to impose Protestantism (alongside efforts to introduce the English system of laws about the inheritance of land) led to rebellion from the Irish chieftains, and much brutal fighting followed.

During the reign of Henry VIII, Wales became formally united with England by the Act for the Government of Wales. The Welsh sent representatives to the House of Commons and the Welsh legal system was reformed.

Henry VIII was succeeded by his son Edward VI, who was strongly Protestant. During his reign, the Book of Common Prayer was written to be used in the Church of England. A version of this book is still used in some churches today. Edward died at the age of 15 after ruling for just over six years, and his half-sister Mary became queen. Mary was a devout Catholic and persecuted Protestants (for this reason, she became known as 'Bloody Mary'). Mary also died after a short reign and the next monarch was her half-sister, Elizabeth, the daughter of Henry VIII and Anne Boleyn.

QUEEN ELIZABETH I

Elizabeth I was the younger daughter of Henry VIII

Queen Elizabeth I was a Protestant. She re-established the Church of England as the official Church in England. Everyone had to attend their local church and there were laws about the type of religious services and the prayers which could be said, but Elizabeth did not ask about people's real beliefs. She succeeded in finding a balance between the views of Catholics and the more extreme Protestants. In this way, she avoided any serious religious conflict within England. Elizabeth became one of the most popular monarchs in English history, particularly after 1588, when the English defeated the Spanish Armada (a large fleet of ships), which had been sent by Spain to conquer England and restore Catholicism.

THE REFORMATION IN SCOTLAND AND MARY, QUEEN OF SCOTS

Scotland had also been strongly influenced by Protestant ideas. In 1560, the predominantly Protestant Scottish Parliament abolished the authority of the Pope in Scotland and Roman Catholic religious services became illegal. A Protestant Church of Scotland with an elected leadership was established but, unlike in England, this was not a state Church.

The queen of Scotland, Mary Stuart (often now called 'Mary, Queen of Scots') was a Catholic. She was only a week old when her father died and she became queen. Much of her childhood was spent in France. When she returned to Scotland, she was the centre of a power struggle between different groups. When her husband was murdered, Mary was suspected of involvement and fled to England. She gave her throne to her Protestant son, James VI of Scotland. Mary was Elizabeth I's cousin and hoped that Elizabeth might help her, but Elizabeth suspected Mary of wanting to take over the English throne, and kept her a prisoner for 20 years. Mary was eventually executed, accused of plotting against Elizabeth I.

> **"**
> 1560, the predominantly Protestant Scottish Parliament abolished the authority of the Pope in Scotland and Roman Catholic religious services became illegal.
> **"**

EXPLORATION, POETRY AND DRAMA

The Elizabethan period in England was a time of growing patriotism: a feeling of pride in being English. English explorers sought new trade routes and tried to expand British trade into the Spanish colonies in the Americas. Sir Francis Drake, one of the commanders in the defeat of the Spanish Armada, was one of the founders of England's naval tradition. His ship, the *Golden Hind*, was one of the first to sail right around ('circumnavigate') the world. In Elizabeth I's time, English settlers first began to colonise the eastern coast of America. This colonisation, particularly by people who disagreed with the religious views of the next two kings, greatly increased in the next century.

The Elizabethan period is also remembered for the richness of its poetry and drama, especially the plays and poems of William Shakespeare.

Shakespeare is widely regarded as the greatest writer in the English language

WILLIAM SHAKESPEARE (1564–1616)

Shakespeare was born in Stratford-upon-Avon, England. He was a playwright and actor and wrote many poems and plays. His most famous plays include *A Midsummer Night's Dream, Hamlet, Macbeth* and *Romeo and Juliet*. He also dramatised significant events from the past, but he did not focus solely on kings and queens. He was one of the first to portray ordinary Englishmen and women. Shakespeare had a great influence on the English language and invented many words that are still common today. Lines from his plays and poems which are often still quoted include:

- Once more unto the breach (*Henry V*)
- To be or not to be (*Hamlet*)
- A rose by any other name (*Romeo and Juliet*)
- All the world's a stage (*As You Like It*)
- The darling buds of May (*Sonnet 18 – Shall I Compare Thee To a Summer's Day*).

Many people regard Shakespeare as the greatest playwright of all time. His plays and poems are still performed and studied in Britain and other countries today. The Globe Theatre in London is a modern copy of the theatres in which his plays were first performed.

JAMES VI AND I

Elizabeth I never married and so had no children of her own to inherit her throne. When she died in 1603 her heir was her cousin James VI of Scotland. He became King James I of England, Wales and Ireland but Scotland remained a separate country.

THE KING JAMES BIBLE

One achievement of King James' reign was a new translation of the Bible into English. This translation is known as the 'King James Version' or the 'Authorised Version'. It was not the first English Bible but is a version which continues to be used in many Protestant churches today.

IRELAND

During this period, Ireland was an almost completely Catholic country. Henry VII and Henry VIII had extended English control outside the Pale (see page 17) and had established English authority over the whole country. Henry VIII took the title 'King of Ireland'. English laws were introduced and local leaders were expected to follow the instructions of the Lord Lieutenants in Dublin.

During the reigns of Elizabeth I and James I, many people in Ireland opposed rule by the Protestant government in England. There were a number of rebellions. The English government encouraged Scottish and English Protestants to settle in Ulster, the northern province of Ireland, taking over the land from Catholic landholders. These settlements were known as plantations. Many of the new settlers came from south-west Scotland and other land was given to companies based in London. James later organised similar plantations in several other parts of Ireland. This had serious long-term consequences for the history of England, Scotland and Ireland.

> **66**
> During the reigns of Elizabeth I and James I, many people in Ireland opposed rule by the Protestant government in England.
> **99**

THE RISE OF PARLIAMENT

Elizabeth I was very skilled at managing Parliament. During her reign, she was successful in balancing her wishes and views against those of the House of Lords and those of the House of Commons, which was increasingly Protestant in its views.

James I and his son Charles I were less skilled politically. Both believed in the 'Divine Right of Kings': the idea that the king was directly appointed by God to rule. They thought that the king should be able to act without having to seek approval from Parliament. When Charles I inherited the thrones of England, Wales, Ireland and Scotland, he tried to rule in line with this principle. When he could not get Parliament to agree with his religious and foreign policies, he tried to rule without Parliament at all. For 11 years, he found ways in which to raise money without Parliament's approval but eventually trouble in Scotland meant that he had to recall Parliament.

THE BEGINNING OF THE ENGLISH CIVIL WAR

Charles I wanted the worship of the Church of England to include more ceremony and introduced a revised Prayer Book.

Charles I wanted the worship of the Church of England to include more ceremony and introduced a revised Prayer Book. He tried to impose this Prayer Book on the Presbyterian Church in Scotland and this led to serious unrest. A Scottish army was formed and Charles could not find the money he needed for his own army without the help of Parliament. In 1640, he recalled Parliament to ask it for funds. Many in Parliament were Puritans, a group of Protestants who advocated strict and simple religious doctrine and worship. They did not agree with the king's religious views and disliked his reforms of the Church of England. Parliament refused to give the king the money he asked for, even after the Scottish army invaded England.

Another rebellion began in Ireland because the Roman Catholics in Ireland were afraid of the growing power of the Puritans. Parliament took this opportunity to demand control of the English army – a change that would have transferred substantial power from the king to Parliament. In response, Charles I entered the House of Commons and tried to arrest five parliamentary leaders, but they had been warned and were not there. (No monarch has set foot in the Commons since.) Civil war between the king and Parliament could not now be avoided and began in 1642. The country split into those who supported the king (the Cavaliers) and those who supported Parliament (the Roundheads).

OLIVER CROMWELL AND THE ENGLISH REPUBLIC

The king's army was defeated at the Battles of Marston Moor and Naseby. By 1646, it was clear that Parliament had won the war. Charles was held prisoner by the parliamentary army. He was still unwilling to reach any agreement with Parliament and in 1649 he was executed.

England declared itself a republic, called the Commonwealth. It no longer had a monarch. For a time, it was not totally clear how the country would be governed. For now, the army was in control. One of its generals, Oliver Cromwell, was sent to Ireland, where the revolt which had begun in 1641 still continued and where there was still a Royalist army. Cromwell was successful in establishing the authority of the English Parliament but did this with such violence that even today Cromwell remains a controversial figure in Ireland.

Oliver Cromwell was the leader of the English republic

The Scots had not agreed to the execution of Charles I and declared his son Charles II to be king. He was crowned king of Scotland and led a Scottish army into England. Cromwell defeated this army in the Battles of Dunbar and Worcester. Charles II escaped from Worcester, famously hiding in an oak tree on one occasion, and eventually fled to Europe. Parliament now controlled Scotland as well as England and Wales.

After his campaign in Ireland and victory over Charles II at Worcester, Cromwell was recognised as the leader of the new republic. He was given the title of Lord Protector and ruled until his death in 1658. When Cromwell died, his son, Richard, became Lord Protector in his place but was not able to control the army or the government. Although Britain had been a republic for 11 years, without Oliver Cromwell there was no clear leader or system of government. Many people in the country wanted stability. People began to talk about the need for a king.

THE RESTORATION

In May 1660, Parliament invited Charles II to come back from exile in the Netherlands. He was crowned King Charles II of England, Wales, Scotland and Ireland. Charles II made it clear that he had 'no wish to go on his travels again'. He understood that he could not always do as he wished but would sometimes need to reach agreement with Parliament. Generally, Parliament supported his policies. The Church of England again became the established official Church. Both Roman Catholics and Puritans were kept out of power.

Habeas corpus is Latin for 'you must present the person in court'. The Act guaranteed that no one could be held prisoner unlawfully.

During Charles II's reign, in 1665, there was a major outbreak of plague in London. Thousands of people died, especially in poorer areas. The following year, a great fire destroyed much of the city, including many churches and St Paul's Cathedral. London was rebuilt with a new St Paul's, which was designed by a famous architect, Sir Christopher Wren. Samuel Pepys wrote about these events in a diary which was later published and is still read today.

The Habeas Corpus Act became law in 1679. This was a very important piece of legislation which remains relevant today. Habeas corpus is Latin for 'you must present the person in court'. The Act guaranteed that no one could be held prisoner unlawfully. Every prisoner has a right to a court hearing.

Charles II was interested in science. During his reign, the Royal Society was formed to promote 'natural knowledge'. This is the oldest surviving scientific society in the world. Among its early members were Sir Edmond Halley, who successfully predicted the return of the comet now called Halley's Comet, and Sir Isaac Newton.

ISAAC NEWTON (1643–1727)

Born in Lincolnshire, eastern England, Isaac Newton first became interested in science when he studied at Cambridge University. He became an important figure in the field. His most famous published work was *Philosophiae Naturalis Principia Mathematica* ('Mathematical Principles of Natural Philosophy'), which showed how gravity applied to the whole universe. Newton also discovered that white light is made up of the colours of the rainbow. Many of his discoveries are still important for modern science.

A CATHOLIC KING

Charles II had no legitimate children. He died in 1685 and his brother, James, who was a Roman Catholic, became King James II in England, Wales and Ireland and King James VII of Scotland. James favoured Roman Catholics and allowed them to be army officers, which an Act of Parliament had forbidden. He did not seek to reach agreements with Parliament and arrested some of the bishops of the Church of England. People in England worried that James wanted to make England a Catholic country once more. However, his heirs were his two daughters, who were both firmly Protestant, and people thought that this meant there would soon be a Protestant monarch again. Then, James' wife had a son. Suddenly, it seemed likely that the next monarch would not be a Protestant after all.

> " William defeated James II at the Battle of the Boyne in Ireland in 1690, an event which is still celebrated by some in Northern Ireland today. "

THE GLORIOUS REVOLUTION

James II's elder daughter, Mary, was married to her cousin William of Orange, the Protestant ruler of the Netherlands. In 1688, important Protestants in England asked William to invade England and proclaim himself king. When William reached England, there was no resistance. James fled to France and William took over the throne, becoming William III in England, Wales and Ireland, and William II of Scotland. William ruled jointly with Mary. This event was later called the 'Glorious Revolution' because there was no fighting in England and because it guaranteed the power of Parliament, ending the threat of a monarch ruling on his or her own as he or she wished. James II wanted to regain the throne and invaded Ireland with the help of a French army. William defeated James II at the Battle of the Boyne in Ireland in 1690, an event which is still celebrated by some in Northern Ireland today.

William re-conquered Ireland and James fled back to France. Many restrictions were placed on the Roman Catholic Church in Ireland and Irish Catholics were unable to take part in the government.

There was also support for James in Scotland. An attempt at an armed rebellion in support of James was quickly defeated at Killiecrankie. All Scottish clans were required formally to accept William as king by taking an oath. The MacDonalds of Glencoe were late in taking the oath and were all killed. The memory of this massacre meant some Scots distrusted the new government.

These kings were known by different titles in Scotland compared to the rest of the Union

Kings of England and Scotland	
England, Wales and Ireland	**Scotland**
James I	James VI
James II	James VII
William III	William II

Some continued to believe that James was the rightful king, particularly in Scotland. Some joined him in exile in France; others were secret supporters. James' supporters became known as Jacobites.

Check that you understand:

- How and why religion changed during this period
- The importance of poetry and drama in the Elizabethan period
- About the involvement of Britain in Ireland
- The development of Parliament and the only period in history when England was a republic
- Why there was a restoration of the monarchy
- How the Glorious Revolution happened

A global power

CONSTITUTIONAL MONARCHY – THE BILL OF RIGHTS

At the coronation of William and Mary, a Declaration of Rights was read. This confirmed that the king would no longer be able to raise taxes or administer justice without agreement from Parliament. The balance of power between monarch and Parliament had now permanently changed. The Bill of Rights, 1689, confirmed the rights of Parliament and the limits of the king's power. Parliament took control of who could be monarch and declared that the king or queen must be a Protestant. A new Parliament had to be elected at least every three years (later this became seven years and now it is five years). Every year the monarch had to ask Parliament to renew funding for the army and the navy.

These changes meant that, to be able to govern effectively, the monarch needed to have advisers, or ministers, who would be able to ensure a majority of votes in the House of Commons and the House of Lords. There were two main groups in Parliament, known as the Whigs and the Tories. (The modern Conservative Party is still sometimes referred to as the Tories.) This was the beginning of party politics.

This was also an important time for the development of a free press (newspapers and other publications which are not controlled by the government). From 1695, newspapers were allowed to operate without a government licence. Increasing numbers of newspapers began to be published.

The laws passed after the Glorious Revolution are the beginning of what is called 'constitutional monarchy'. The monarch remained very important but was no longer able to insist on particular policies or actions if Parliament did not agree. After William III, the ministers gradually became more important than the monarch but this was not a democracy in the modern sense. The number of people who had the right to vote for members of Parliament was still very small. Only men who owned property of a certain value were able to vote. No women at all had the vote. Some constituencies were controlled by a single wealthy family. These were called 'pocket boroughs'. Other constituencies had hardly any voters and were called 'rotten boroughs'.

> " The Bill of Rights, 1689, confirmed the rights of Parliament and the limits of the king's power. "

A GROWING POPULATION

This was a time when many people left Britain and Ireland to settle in new colonies in America and elsewhere, but others came to live in Britain. The first Jews to come to Britain since the Middle Ages settled in London in 1656. Between 1680 and 1720 many refugees called Huguenots came from France. They were Protestants and had been persecuted for their religion. Many were educated and skilled and worked as scientists, in banking, or in weaving or other crafts.

THE ACT OR TREATY OF UNION IN SCOTLAND

William and Mary's successor, Queen Anne, had no surviving children. This created uncertainty over the succession in England, Wales and Ireland and in Scotland. The Act of Union, known as the Treaty of Union in Scotland, was therefore agreed in 1707, creating the Kingdom of Great Britain. Although Scotland was no longer an independent country, it kept its own legal and education systems and Presbyterian Church.

> The Act of Union, known as the Treaty of Union in Scotland, was agreed in 1707, creating the Kingdom of Great Britain.

THE PRIME MINISTER

When Queen Anne died in 1714, Parliament chose a German, George I, to be the next king, because he was Anne's nearest Protestant relative. An attempt by Scottish Jacobites to put James II's son on the throne instead was quickly defeated. George I did not speak very good English and this increased his need to rely on his ministers. The most important minister in Parliament became known as the Prime Minister. The first man to be called this was Sir Robert Walpole, who was Prime Minister from 1721 to 1742.

THE REBELLION OF THE CLANS

In 1745 there was another attempt to put a Stuart king back on the throne in place of George I's son, George II. Charles Edward Stuart (Bonnie Prince Charlie), the grandson of James II, landed in Scotland. He was supported by clansmen from the Scottish highlands and raised an army. Charles initially had some successes but was defeated by George II's army at the Battle of Culloden in 1746. Charles escaped back to Europe.

The clans lost a lot of their power and influence after Culloden. Chieftains became landlords if they had the favour of the English king, and clansmen became tenants who had to pay for the land they used.

A process began which became known as the 'Highland Clearances'. Many Scottish landlords destroyed individual small farms (known as 'crofts') to make space for large flocks of sheep and cattle. Evictions became very common in the early 19th century. Many Scottish people left for North America at this time.

ROBERT BURNS (1759–96)

Known in Scotland as 'The Bard', Robert Burns was a Scottish poet. He wrote in the Scots language, English with some Scottish words, and standard English. He also revised a lot of traditional folk songs by changing or adding lyrics. Burns' best-known work is probably the song *Auld Lang Syne*, which is sung by people in the UK and other countries when they are celebrating the New Year (or Hogmanay as it is called in Scotland).

THE ENLIGHTENMENT

During the 18th century, new ideas about politics, philosophy and science were developed. This is often called 'the Enlightenment'. Many of the great thinkers of the Enlightenment were Scottish. Adam Smith developed ideas about economics which are still referred to today. David Hume's ideas about human nature continue to influence philosophers. Scientific discoveries, such as James Watt's work on steam power, helped the progress of the Industrial Revolution. One of the most important principles of the Enlightenment was that everyone should have the right to their own political and religious beliefs and that the state should not try to dictate to them. This continues to be an important principle in the UK today.

> " Scientific discoveries, such as James Watt's work on steam power, helped the progress of the Industrial Revolution. "

THE INDUSTRIAL REVOLUTION

Before the 18th century, agriculture was the biggest source of employment in Britain. There were many cottage industries, where people worked from home to produce goods such as cloth and lace.

The Industrial Revolution was the rapid development of industry in Britain in the 18th and 19th centuries. Britain was the first country to industrialise on a large scale. It happened because of the development of machinery and the use of steam power. Agriculture and the manufacturing of goods became mechanised. This made things more efficient and increased production. Coal and other raw materials were needed to power the new factories. Many people moved from the countryside and started working in the mining and manufacturing industries.

The development of the Bessemer process for the mass production of steel led to the development of the shipbuilding industry and the railways. Manufacturing jobs became the main source of employment in Britain.

RICHARD ARKWRIGHT (1732–92)

Born in 1732, Arkwright originally trained and worked as a barber. He was able to dye hair and make wigs. When wigs became less popular, he started to work in textiles. He improved the original carding machine. Carding is the process of preparing fibres for spinning into yarn and fabric. He also developed horse-driven spinning mills that used only one machine. This increased the efficiency of production. Later, he used the steam engine to power machinery. Arkwright is particularly remembered for the efficient and profitable way that he ran his factories.

?

You may be asked about key historical figures and their work. Focus on what their achievements meant for Britain, for example how Arkwright made the textile industry more efficient.

Richard Arkwright's carding machine

© SSPL via Getty Images

Better transport links were needed to transport raw materials and manufactured goods. Canals were built to link the factories to towns and cities and to the ports, particularly in the new industrial areas in the middle and north of England.

Working conditions during the Industrial Revolution were very poor. There were no laws to protect employees, who were often forced to work long hours in dangerous situations. Children also worked and were treated in the same way as adults. Sometimes they were treated even more harshly.

This was also a time of increased colonisation overseas. Captain James Cook mapped the coast of Australia and a few colonies were established there. Britain gained control over Canada, and the East India Company, originally set up to trade, gained control of large parts of India. Colonies began to be established in southern Africa.

Britain traded all over the world and began to import more goods. Sugar and tobacco came from North America and the West Indies; textiles, tea and spices came from India and the area that is today called Indonesia. Trading and settlements overseas sometimes brought Britain into conflict with other countries, particularly France, which was expanding and trading in a similar way in many of the same areas of the world.

SAKE DEAN MAHOMET (1759–1851)

Mahomet was born in 1759 and grew up in the Bengal region of India. He served in the Bengal army and came to Britain in 1782. He then moved to Ireland and eloped with an Irish girl called Jane Daly in 1786, returning to England at the turn of the century. In 1810 he opened the Hindoostane Coffee House in George Street, London. It was the first curry house to open in Britain. Mahomet and his wife also introduced 'shampooing', the Indian art of head massage, to Britain.

Despite being called The Hindoostane **Coffee** House, it was indeed one of the first **curry** houses in the UK. This text is correct.

THE SLAVE TRADE

This commercial expansion and prosperity was sustained in part by the booming slave trade. While slavery was illegal within Britain itself, by the 18th century it was a fully established overseas industry, dominated by Britain and the American colonies.

Slaves came primarily from West Africa. Travelling on British ships in horrible conditions, they were taken to America and the

Caribbean, where they were made to work on tobacco and sugar plantations. The living and working conditions for slaves were very bad. Many slaves tried to escape and others revolted against their owners in protest at their terrible treatment.

There were, however, people in Britain who opposed the slave trade. The first formal anti-slavery groups were set up by the Quakers in the late 1700s, and they petitioned Parliament to ban the practice. William Wilberforce, an evangelical Christian and a member of Parliament, also played an important part in changing the law. Along with other abolitionists (people who supported the abolition of slavery), he succeeded in turning public opinion against the slave trade. In 1807, it became illegal to trade slaves in British ships or from British ports, and in 1833 the Emancipation Act abolished slavery throughout the British Empire. The Royal Navy stopped slave ships from other countries, freed the slaves and punished the slave traders. After 1833, 2 million Indian and Chinese workers were employed to replace the freed slaves. They worked on sugar plantations in the Caribbean, in mines in South Africa, on railways in East Africa and in the army in Kenya.

In 1807, it became illegal to trade slaves in British ships or from British ports, and in 1833 the Emancipation Act abolished slavery throughout the British Empire.

THE AMERICAN WAR OF INDEPENDENCE

By the 1760s, there were substantial British colonies in North America. The colonies were wealthy and largely in control of their own affairs. Many of the colonist families had originally gone to North America in order to have religious freedom. They were well educated and interested in ideas of liberty. The British government wanted to tax the colonies. The colonists saw this as an attack on their freedom and said there should be 'no taxation without representation' in the British Parliament. Parliament tried to compromise by repealing some of the taxes, but relationships between the British government and the colonies continued to worsen. Fighting broke out between the colonists and the British forces. In 1776, 13 American colonies declared their independence, stating that people had a right to establish their own governments. The colonists eventually defeated the British army and Britain recognised the colonies' independence in 1783.

WAR WITH FRANCE

During the 18th century, Britain fought a number of wars with France. In 1789, there was a revolution in France and the new French government soon declared war on Britain. Napoleon, who became Emperor of France, continued the war. Britain's navy fought against combined French and Spanish fleets, winning the Battle of Trafalgar in 1805. Admiral Nelson was in charge of the British fleet at Trafalgar and was killed in the battle. Nelson's Column in Trafalgar Square, London, is a monument to him. His ship, *HMS Victory*, can be visited in Portsmouth. The British army also fought against the French. In 1815, the French Wars ended with the defeat of the Emperor Napoleon by the Duke of Wellington at the Battle of Waterloo. Wellington was known as the Iron Duke and later became Prime Minister.

The Battle of Trafalgar (21 October 1805) was a naval engagement fought by the British Royal Navy against the combined fleets of the French Navy and Spanish Navy

THE UNION FLAG

Although Ireland had had the same monarch as England and Wales since Henry VIII, it had remained a separate country. In 1801, Ireland became unified with England, Scotland and Wales after the Act of Union of 1800. This created the United Kingdom of Great Britain and Ireland. One symbol of this union between England, Scotland, Wales and Ireland was a new version of the official flag, the Union Flag. This is often called the Union Jack. The flag combined crosses associated with England, Scotland and Ireland. It is still used today as the official flag of the UK.

The Union Flag consists of three crosses:

- The cross of St George, patron saint of England, is a red cross on a white ground.
- The cross of St Andrew, patron saint of Scotland, is a diagonal white cross on a blue ground.
- The cross of St Patrick, patron saint of Ireland, is a diagonal red cross on a white ground.

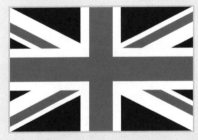

The Union Flag, also known as the Union Jack

The crosses of the three countries which combined to form the Union Flag

The cross of St George   *The cross of St Andrew*   *The cross of St Patrick*

There is also an official Welsh flag, which shows a Welsh dragon. The Welsh dragon does not appear on the Union Flag because, when the first Union Flag was created in 1606 from the flags of Scotland and England, the Principality of Wales was already united with England.

The official Welsh flag

THE VICTORIAN AGE

In 1837, Queen Victoria became queen of the UK at the age of 18. She reigned until 1901, almost 64 years. At the date of writing (2013) this is the longest reign of any British monarch. Her reign is known as the Victorian Age. It was a time when Britain increased in power and influence abroad. Within the UK, the middle classes became increasingly significant and a number of reformers led moves to improve conditions of life for the poor.

THE BRITISH EMPIRE

During the Victorian period, the British Empire grew to cover all of India, Australia and large parts of Africa. It became the largest empire the world has ever seen, with an estimated population of more than 400 million people.

Many people were encouraged to leave the UK to settle overseas. Between 1853 and 1913, as many as 13 million British citizens left the country. People continued to come to Britain from other parts of the world. For example, between 1870 and 1914, around 120,000 Russian and Polish Jews came to Britain to escape persecution. Many settled in London's East End and in Manchester and Leeds. People from the Empire, including India and Africa, also came to Britain to live, work and study.

TRADE AND INDUSTRY

Britain continued to be a great trading nation. The government began to promote policies of free trade, abolishing a number of taxes on imported goods. One example of this was the repealing of the Corn Laws in 1846. These had prevented the import of cheap grain. The reforms helped the development of British industry, because raw materials could now be imported more cheaply.

Working conditions in factories gradually became better. In 1847, the number of hours that women and children could work was limited by law to 10 hours per day. Better housing began to be built for workers.

Transport links also improved, enabling goods and people to move more easily around the country. Just before Victoria came to the throne, the father and son George and Robert Stephenson pioneered the railway engine and a major expansion of the railways took place in the Victorian period. Railways were built throughout the Empire. There were also great advances in other

> Elizabeth II became the UK's longest reigning monarch in September 2015. For the purposes of your test you should learn the material as reproduced here.

> Between 1853 and 1913, as many as 13 million British citizens left the country.

areas, such as the building of bridges by engineers such as Isambard Kingdom Brunel.

ISAMBARD KINGDOM BRUNEL (1806–59)

Brunel was originally from Portsmouth, England. He was an engineer who built tunnels, bridges, railway lines and ships. He was responsible for constructing the Great Western Railway, which was the first major railway built in Britain. It runs from Paddington Station in London to the south west of England, the West Midlands and Wales. Many of Brunel's bridges are still in use today.

The Clifton Suspension Bridge, designed by Isambard Kingdom Brunel, spanning the Avon Gorge

British industry led the world in the 19th century. The UK produced more than half of the world's iron, coal and cotton cloth. The UK also became a centre for financial services, including insurance and banking. In 1851, the Great Exhibition opened in Hyde Park in the Crystal Palace, a huge building made of steel and glass. Exhibits ranged from huge machines to handmade goods. Countries from all over the world showed their goods but most of the objects were made in Britain.

THE CRIMEAN WAR

From 1853 to 1856, Britain fought with Turkey and France against Russia in the Crimean War. It was the first war to be extensively covered by the media through news stories and photographs. The conditions were very poor and many soldiers died from illnesses they caught in the hospitals, rather than from war wounds. Queen Victoria introduced the Victoria Cross medal during this war. It honours acts of valour by soldiers.

FLORENCE NIGHTINGALE (1820–1910)

Florence Nightingale was born in Italy to English parents. At the age of 31, she trained as a nurse in Germany. In 1854, she went to Turkey and worked in military hospitals, treating soldiers who were fighting in the Crimean War. She and her fellow nurses improved the conditions in the hospital and reduced the mortality rate. In 1860 she established the Nightingale Training School for nurses at St Thomas' Hospital in London. The school was the first of its kind and still exists today, as do many of the practices that Florence used. She is often regarded as the founder of modern nursing.

IRELAND IN THE 19TH CENTURY

Conditions in Ireland were not as good as in the rest of the UK. Two-thirds of the population still depended on farming to make their living, often on very small plots of land. Many depended on potatoes as a large part of their diet. In the middle of the century the potato crop failed, and Ireland suffered a famine. A million people died from disease and starvation. Another million and a half left Ireland. Some emigrated to the United States and others came to England. By 1861 there were large populations of Irish people in cities such as Liverpool, London, Manchester and Glasgow.

The Irish Nationalist movement had grown strongly through the 19th century. Some, such as the Fenians, favoured complete independence. Others, such as Charles Stuart Parnell, advocated 'Home Rule', in which Ireland would remain in the UK but have its own parliament.

> **"** By 1861 there were large populations of Irish people in cities such as Liverpool, London, Manchester and Glasgow. **"**

THE RIGHT TO VOTE

As the middle classes in the wealthy industrial towns and cities grew in influence, they began to demand more political power. The Reform Act of 1832 had greatly increased the number of people with the right to vote. The Act also abolished the old pocket and rotten boroughs (see page 33) and more parliamentary seats were given to the towns and cities. There was a permanent shift of political power from the countryside to the towns but voting was still based on ownership of property. This meant that members of the working class were still unable to vote.

A movement began to demand the vote for the working classes and other people without property. Campaigners, called the Chartists, presented petitions to Parliament. At first they seemed to be unsuccessful, but in 1867 there was another Reform Act. This created many more urban seats in Parliament and reduced the amount of property that people needed to have before they could vote. However, the majority of men still did not have the right to vote and no women could vote.

Politicians realised that the increased number of voters meant that they needed to persuade people to vote for them if they were to be sure of being elected to Parliament. The political parties began to create organisations to reach out to ordinary voters. Universal suffrage (the right of every adult, male or female, to vote) followed in the next century.

In common with the rest of Europe, women in 19th-century Britain had fewer rights than men. Until 1870, when a woman got married, her earnings, property and money automatically belonged to her husband. Acts of Parliament in 1870 and 1882 gave wives the right to keep their own earnings and property. In the late 19th and early 20th centuries, an increasing number of women campaigned and demonstrated for greater rights and, in particular, the right to vote. They formed the women's suffrage movement and became known as 'suffragettes'.

> In 1867 there was another Reform Act. This created many more urban seats in Parliament and reduced the amount of property that people needed to have before they could vote.

EMMELINE PANKHURST (1858–1928)

Emmeline Pankhurst was born in Manchester in 1858. She set up the Women's Franchise League in 1889, which fought to get the vote in local elections for married women. In 1903 she helped found the Women's Social and Political Union (WSPU). This was the first group whose members were called 'suffragettes'. The group used civil disobedience as part of their protest to gain the vote for women. They chained themselves to railings, smashed windows and committed arson. Many of the women, including Emmeline, went on hunger strike. In 1918, women over the age of 30 were given voting rights and the right to stand for Parliament, partly in recognition of the contribution women made to the war effort during the First World War. Shortly before Emmeline's death in 1928, women were given the right to vote at the age of 21, the same as men.

THE FUTURE OF THE EMPIRE

Although the British Empire continued to grow until the 1920s, there was already discussion in the late 19th century about its future direction. Supporters of expansion believed that the Empire benefited Britain through increased trade and commerce. Others thought the Empire had become over-expanded and that the frequent conflicts in many parts of the Empire, such as India's north-west frontier or southern Africa, were a drain on resources. Yet the great majority of British people believed in the Empire as a force for good in the world.

The Boer War of 1899 to 1902 made the discussions about the future of the Empire more urgent. The British went to war in South Africa with settlers from the Netherlands called the Boers. The Boers fought fiercely and the war went on for over three years. Many died in the fighting and many more from disease. There was some public sympathy for the Boers and people began to question whether the Empire could continue. As different parts of the Empire developed, they won greater freedom and autonomy from Britain. Eventually, by the second half of the 20th century, there was, for the most part, an orderly transition from Empire to Commonwealth, with countries being granted their independence.

The Boer War of 1899 to 1902 made the discussions about the future of the Empire more urgent.

RUDYARD KIPLING (1865–1936)

Rudyard Kipling was born in India in 1865 and later lived in India, the UK and the USA. He wrote books and poems set in both India and the UK. His poems and novels reflected the idea that the British Empire was a force for good. Kipling was awarded the Nobel Prize in Literature in 1907. His books include the *Just So Stories* and *The Jungle Book*, which continue to be popular today. His poem *If* has often been voted among the UK's favourite poems. It begins with these words:

'If you can keep your head when all about you
Are losing theirs and blaming it on you;
If you can trust yourself when all men doubt you,
But make allowance for their doubting too;
If you can wait and not be tired by waiting,
Or being lied about, don't deal in lies,
Or being hated, don't give way to hating,
And yet don't look too good, nor talk too wise'
(*If*, Rudyard Kipling)

Check that you understand:

- The change in the balance of power between Parliament and the monarchy
- When and why Scotland joined England and Wales to become Great Britain
- The reasons for a rebellion in Scotland led by Bonnie Prince Charlie
- The ideas of the Enlightenment
- The importance of the Industrial Revolution and development of industry
- The slave trade and when it was abolished
- The growth of the British Empire
- How democracy developed during this period

The 20th century

THE FIRST WORLD WAR

On 28 June 1914, Archduke Franz Ferdinand of Austria was assassinated. This set off a chain of events leading to the First World War (1914–18).

The early 20th century was a time of optimism in Britain. The nation, with its expansive Empire, well-admired navy, thriving industry and strong political institutions, was what is now known as a global 'superpower'. It was also a time of social progress. Financial help for the unemployed, old-age pensions and free school meals were just a few of the important measures introduced. Various laws were passed to improve safety in the workplace; town planning rules were tightened to prevent the further development of slums; and better support was given to mothers and their children after divorce or separation. Local government became more democratic and a salary for members of Parliament (MPs) was introduced for the first time, making it easier for more people to take part in public life.

This era of optimism and progress was cut short when war broke out between several European nations. On 28 June 1914, Archduke Franz Ferdinand of Austria was assassinated. This set off a chain of events leading to the First World War (1914–18). But while the assassination provided the trigger for war, other factors – such as a growing sense of nationalism in many European states; increasing militarism; imperialism; and the division of the major European powers into two camps – all set the conditions for war.

The conflict was centred in Europe, but it was a global war involving nations from around the world. Britain was part of the Allied Powers, which included (amongst others) France, Russia, Japan, Belgium, Serbia – and later, Greece, Italy, Romania and the United States. The whole of the British Empire was involved in the conflict – for example, more than a million Indians fought on behalf of Britain in lots of different countries, and around 40,000 were killed. Men from the West Indies, Africa, Australia, New Zealand and Canada also fought with the British. The Allies fought against the Central Powers – mainly Germany, the Austro-Hungarian Empire, the Ottoman Empire and later Bulgaria. Millions of people were killed or wounded, with more than 2 million British casualties. One battle, the British attack on the Somme in July 1916, resulted in about 60,000 British casualties on the first day alone.

The British attack on the Somme in July 1916 resulted in about 60,000 British casualties on the first day alone.

Soldiers fighting in the trenches during the First World War

© Popperfoto/Getty Images

The First World War ended at 11.00 am on 11 November 1918 with victory for Britain and its allies.

THE PARTITION OF IRELAND

In 1913, the British government promised 'Home Rule' for Ireland. The proposal was to have a self-governing Ireland with its own parliament but still part of the UK. A Home Rule Bill was introduced in Parliament. It was opposed by the Protestants in the north of Ireland, who threatened to resist Home Rule by force.

The outbreak of the First World War led the British government to postpone any changes in Ireland. Irish Nationalists were not willing to wait and in 1916 there was an uprising (the Easter Rising) against the British in Dublin. The leaders of the uprising were executed under military law. A guerrilla war against the British army and the police in Ireland followed. In 1921 a peace treaty was signed and in 1922 Ireland became two countries. The six counties in the north which were mainly Protestant remained part of the UK under the name Northern Ireland. The rest of Ireland became the Irish Free State. It had its own government and became a republic in 1949.

There were people in both parts of Ireland who disagreed with the split between the North and the South. They still wanted Ireland to be one independent country. Years of disagreement led to a terror campaign in Northern Ireland and elsewhere. The conflict between those wishing for full Irish independence and those wishing to remain loyal to the British government is often referred to as 'the Troubles'.

Car ownership doubled from 1 million to 2 million between 1930 and 1939. In addition, many new houses were built.

THE INTER-WAR PERIOD

In the 1920s, many people's living conditions got better. There were improvements in public housing and new homes were built in many towns and cities. However, in 1929, the world entered the 'Great Depression' and some parts of the UK suffered mass unemployment. The effects of the depression of the 1930s were felt differently in different parts of the UK. The traditional heavy industries such as shipbuilding were badly affected but new industries – including the automobile and aviation industries – developed. As prices generally fell, those in work had more money to spend. Car ownership doubled from 1 million to 2 million between 1930 and 1939. In addition, many new houses were built. It was also a time of cultural blossoming, with writers such as Graham Greene and Evelyn Waugh prominent. The economist John Maynard Keynes published influential new theories of economics. The BBC started radio broadcasts in 1922 and began the world's first regular television service in 1936.

THE SECOND WORLD WAR

Adolf Hitler came to power in Germany in 1933. He believed that the conditions imposed on Germany by the Allies after the First World War were unfair; he also wanted to conquer more land for the German people. He set about renegotiating treaties, building up arms, and testing Germany's military strength in nearby countries. The British government tried to avoid another war. However, when Hitler invaded Poland in 1939, Britain and France declared war in order to stop his aggression.

The war was initially fought between the Axis powers (fascist Germany and Italy and the Empire of Japan) and the Allies. The main countries on the allied side were the UK, France, Poland, Australia, New Zealand, Canada, and the Union of South Africa.

Having occupied Austria and invaded Czechoslovakia, Hitler followed his invasion of Poland by taking control of Belgium and the Netherlands. Then, in 1940, German forces defeated allied troops and advanced through France. At this time of national crisis, Winston Churchill became Prime Minister and Britain's war leader.

As France fell, the British decided to evacuate British and French soldiers from France in a huge naval operation. Many civilian volunteers in small pleasure and fishing boats from Britain helped the Navy to rescue more than 300,000 men from the beaches around Dunkirk. Although many lives and a lot of equipment were lost, the evacuation was a success and meant that Britain was better able to continue the fight against the Germans. The evacuation gave rise to the phrase 'the Dunkirk spirit'.

From the end of June 1940 until the German invasion of the Soviet Union in June 1941, Britain and the Empire stood almost alone against Nazi Germany.

Hitler wanted to invade Britain, but before sending in troops, Germany needed to control the air. The Germans waged an air campaign against Britain, but the British resisted with their fighter planes and eventually won the crucial aerial battle against the Germans, called 'the Battle of Britain', in the summer of 1940. The most important planes used by the Royal Air Force in the Battle of Britain were the Spitfire and the Hurricane – which were designed and built in Britain. Despite this crucial victory, the German air force was able to continue bombing London and other British cities at night-time. This was called the Blitz. Coventry was almost totally destroyed and a great deal of damage was done in other cities, especially in the East End of London. Despite the destruction, there was a strong national spirit of resistance in the UK. The phrase 'the Blitz spirit' is still used today to describe Britons pulling together in the face of adversity.

Many civilian volunteers in small pleasure and fishing boats from Britain helped the Navy to rescue more than 300,000 men from the beaches around Dunkirk.

Make sure you know the planes used in the Battle of Britain, and which parts of the UK were most affected by the Blitz.

Winston Churchill, best known for his leadership of the UK during the Second World War

© Richard Baker/In Pictures/Corbis

WINSTON CHURCHILL (1874–1965)

Churchill was the son of a politician and, before becoming a Conservative MP in 1900, was a soldier and journalist. In May 1940 he became Prime Minister. He refused to surrender to the Nazis and was an inspirational leader to the British people in a time of great hardship. He lost the General Election in 1945 but returned as Prime Minister in 1951.

He was an MP until he stood down at the 1964 General Election. Following his death in 1965, he was given a state funeral. He remains a much-admired figure to this day, and in 2002 was voted the greatest Briton of all time by the public. During the War, he made many famous speeches including lines which you may still hear:

> *'I have nothing to offer but blood, toil, tears and sweat'*

Churchill's first speech to the House of Commons after he became Prime Minister, 1940

> *'We shall fight on the beaches,*
> *we shall fight on the landing grounds,*
> *we shall fight in the fields and in the streets,*
> *we shall fight in the hills;*
> *we shall never surrender'*

Speech to the House of Commons after Dunkirk (see above), 1940

> *'Never in the field of human conflict was so much owed by so many to so few'*

Speech to the House of Commons during the Battle of Britain (see above), 1940

?

You may be asked to identify famous quotes from speeches by people such as Churchill. Make sure you know who said what.

At the same time as defending Britain, the British military was fighting the Axis on many other fronts. In Singapore, the Japanese defeated the British and then occupied Burma, threatening India. The United States entered the war when the Japanese bombed its naval base at Pearl Harbor in December 1941.

That same year, Hitler attempted the largest invasion in history by attacking the Soviet Union. It was a fierce conflict, with huge losses on both sides. German forces were ultimately repelled by the Soviets, and the damage they sustained proved to be a pivotal point in the war.

The Royal Air Force helped to defend Britain in the Second World War

© Getty Images

The allied forces gradually gained the upper hand, winning significant victories in North Africa and Italy. German losses in the Soviet Union, combined with the support of the Americans, meant that the Allies were eventually strong enough to attack Hitler's forces in Western Europe. On 6 June 1944, allied forces landed in Normandy (this event is often referred to as 'D-Day'). Following victory on the beaches of Normandy, the allied forces pressed on through France and eventually into Germany. The Allies comprehensively defeated Germany in May 1945.

The war against Japan ended in August 1945 when the United States dropped its newly developed atom bombs on the Japanese cities of Hiroshima and Nagasaki. Scientists led by Ernest Rutherford, working at Manchester and then Cambridge University, were the first to 'split the atom' and took part in the Manhattan Project in the United States, which developed the atomic bomb. The war was finally over.

ALEXANDER FLEMING (1881–1955)

Born in Scotland, Fleming moved to London as a teenager and later qualified as a doctor. He was researching influenza (the 'flu') in 1928 when he discovered penicillin. This was then further developed into a usable drug by the scientists Howard Florey and Ernst Chain. By the 1940s it was in mass production. Fleming won the Nobel Prize in Medicine in 1945. Penicillin is still used to treat bacterial infections today.

Check that you understand:

- What happened during the First World War
- The partition of Ireland and the establishment of the UK as it is today
- The events of the Second World War

 Britain since 1945

In 1948, Aneurin (Nye) Bevan, the Minister for Health, led the establishment of the National Health Service (NHS), which guaranteed a minimum standard of health care for all, free at the point of use.

THE WELFARE STATE

Although the UK had won the war, the country was exhausted economically and the people wanted change. During the war, there had been significant reforms to the education system and people now looked for wider social reforms.

In 1945 the British people elected a Labour government. The new Prime Minister was Clement Atlee, who promised to introduce the welfare state outlined in the Beveridge Report. In 1948, Aneurin (Nye) Bevan, the Minister for Health, led the establishment of the National Health Service (NHS), which guaranteed a minimum standard of health care for all, free at the point of use. A national system of benefits was also introduced to provide 'social security', so that the population would be protected from the 'cradle to the grave'. The government took into public ownership (nationalised) the railways, coal mines and gas, water and electricity supplies.

Another aspect of change was self-government for former colonies. In 1947, independence was granted to nine countries, including India, Pakistan and Ceylon (now Sri Lanka). Other colonies in Africa, the Caribbean and the Pacific achieved independence over the next 20 years.

The UK developed its own atomic bomb and joined the new North Atlantic Treaty Organization (NATO), an alliance of nations set up to resist the perceived threat of invasion by the Soviet Union and its allies.

Britain had a Conservative government from 1951 to 1964. The 1950s was a period of economic recovery after the war and increasing prosperity for working people. The Prime Minister of the day, Harold Macmillan, was famous for his 'wind of change' speech about decolonisation and independence for the countries of the Empire.

CLEMENT ATTLEE (1883–1967)

Clement Attlee was born in London in 1883. His father was a solicitor and, after studying at Oxford University, Attlee became a barrister. He gave this up to do social work in East London and eventually became a Labour MP. He was Winston Churchill's Deputy Prime Minister in the wartime coalition government and became Prime Minister after the Labour Party won the 1945 election. He was Prime Minister from 1945 to 1951 and led the Labour Party for 20 years. Attlee's government undertook the nationalisation of major industries (like coal and steel), created the National Health Service and implemented many of Beveridge's plans for a stronger welfare state. Attlee also introduced measures to improve the conditions of workers.

You may be asked questions about the formation of the welfare state. Take some time to study the key figures and how they contributed to it, as well as key reports and legislation.

WILLIAM BEVERIDGE (1879–1963)

William Beveridge (later Lord Beveridge) was a British economist and social reformer. He served briefly as a Liberal MP and was subsequently the leader of the Liberals in the House of Lords but is best known for the 1942 report *Social Insurance and Allied Services* (known as the Beveridge Report). The report was commissioned by the wartime government in 1941. It recommended that the government should find ways of fighting the five 'Giant Evils' of Want, Disease, Ignorance, Squalor and Idleness and provided the basis of the modern welfare state.

R A BUTLER (1902–82)

Richard Austen Butler (later Lord Butler) was born in 1902. He became a Conservative MP in 1923 and held several positions before becoming responsible for education in 1941. In this role, he oversaw the introduction of the Education Act 1944 (often called 'The Butler Act'), which introduced free secondary education in England and Wales. The education system has changed significantly since the Act was introduced, but the division between primary and secondary schools that it enforced still remains in most areas of Britain.

DYLAN THOMAS (1914–53)

Dylan Thomas was a Welsh poet and writer. He often read and performed his work in public, including for the BBC. His most well-known works include the radio play *Under Milk Wood*, first performed after his death in 1954, and the poem *Do Not Go Gentle into That Good Night*, which he wrote for his dying father in 1952. He died at the age of 39 in New York. There are several memorials to him in his birthplace, Swansea, including a statue and the Dylan Thomas Centre.

MIGRATION IN POST-WAR BRITAIN

Rebuilding Britain after the Second World War was a huge task. There were labour shortages and the British government encouraged workers from Ireland and other parts of Europe to come to the UK and help with the reconstruction. In 1948, people from the West Indies were also invited to come and work.

During the 1950s, there was still a shortage of labour in the UK. Further immigration was therefore encouraged for economic reasons, and many industries advertised for workers from overseas. For example, centres were set up in the West Indies to recruit people to drive buses. Textile and engineering firms from the north of England and the Midlands sent agents to India and Pakistan to find workers. For about 25 years, people from the West Indies, India, Pakistan and (later) Bangladesh travelled to work and settle in Britain.

SOCIAL CHANGE IN THE 1960s

The decade of the 1960s was a period of significant social change. It was known as 'the Swinging Sixties'. There was growth in British fashion, cinema and popular music. Two well-known pop music groups at the time were The Beatles and The Rolling Stones. People started to become better off and many bought cars and other consumer goods.

It was also a time when social laws were liberalised, for example in relation to divorce and to abortion in England, Wales and Scotland. The position of women in the workplace also improved. It was quite common at the time for employers to ask women to leave their jobs when they got married, but Parliament passed new laws giving women the right to equal pay and made it illegal for employers to discriminate against women because of their gender.

The 1960s was also a time of technological progress. Britain and France developed the world's only supersonic commercial airliner, Concorde. New styles of architecture, including high-rise buildings and the use of concrete and steel, became common.

The number of people migrating from the West Indies, India, Pakistan and what is now Bangladesh fell in the late 1960s because the government passed new laws to restrict immigration to Britain. Immigrants were required to have a strong connection to Britain through birth or ancestry. Even so, during the early 1970s, Britain admitted 28,000 people of Indian origin who had been forced to leave Uganda.

There was another supersonic commercial airliner called the Tupolev Tu-144 which flew passenger flights between 1977–78. However, for the purposes of your test you should learn the material as reproduced here.

SOME GREAT BRITISH INVENTIONS OF THE 20TH CENTURY

Britain has given the world some wonderful inventions. Examples from the 20th century include:

The **television** was developed by Scotsman John Logie Baird (1888–1946) in the 1920s. In 1932 he made the first television broadcast between London and Glasgow.

Radar was developed by Scotsman Sir Robert Watson-Watt (1892–1973), who proposed that enemy aircraft could be detected by radio waves. The first successful radar test took place in 1935.

Working with radar led Sir Bernard Lovell (1913–2012) to make new discoveries in astronomy. The radio telescope he built at **Jodrell Bank** in Cheshire was for many years the biggest in the world and continues to operate today.

A **Turing machine** is a theoretical mathematical device invented by Alan Turing (1912–54), a British mathematician, in the 1930s. The theory was influential in the development of computer science and the modern-day computer.

The Scottish physician and researcher John MacLeod (1876–1935) was the co-discoverer of **insulin**, used to treat diabetes.

The **structure of the DNA molecule** was discovered in 1953 through work at British universities in London and Cambridge. This discovery contributed to many scientific advances, particularly in medicine and fighting crime. Francis Crick (1916–2004), one of those awarded the Nobel Prize for this discovery, was British.

The **jet engine** was developed in Britain in the 1930s by Sir Frank Whittle (1907–96), a British Royal Air Force engineer officer.

Sir Christopher Cockerell (1910–99), a British inventor, invented the **hovercraft** in the 1950s.

Britain and France developed **Concorde**, the world's only supersonic passenger aircraft. It first flew in 1969 and began carrying passengers in 1976. Concorde was retired from service in 2003.

The **Harrier jump jet**, an aircraft capable of taking off vertically, was also designed and developed in the UK.

In the 1960s, James Goodfellow (1937–) invented the **cash-dispensing ATM** (automatic teller machine) or 'cashpoint'. The first of these was put into use by Barclays Bank in Enfield, north London in 1967.

IVF (in-vitro fertilisation) therapy for the treatment of infertility was pioneered in Britain by physiologist Sir Robert Edwards (1925–2013) and gynaecologist Patrick Steptoe (1913–88). The world's first 'test-tube baby' was born in Oldham, Lancashire in 1978.

In 1996, two British scientists, Sir Ian Wilmut (1944–) and Keith Campbell (1954–2012), led a team which was the first to succeed in **cloning** a mammal, Dolly the sheep. This has led to further research into the possible use of cloning to preserve endangered species and for medical purposes.

Sir Peter Mansfield (1933–), a British scientist, is the co-inventor of the **MRI (magnetic resonance imaging)** scanner. This enables doctors and researchers to obtain exact and non-invasive images of human internal organs and has revolutionised diagnostic medicine.

The inventor of the **World Wide Web**, Sir Tim Berners-Lee (1955–), is British. Information was successfully transferred via the web for the first time on 25 December 1990.

PROBLEMS IN THE ECONOMY IN THE 1970s

In the late 1970s, the post-war economic boom came to an end. Prices of goods and raw materials began to rise sharply and the exchange rate between the pound and other currencies was unstable. This caused problems with the 'balance of payments': imports of goods were valued at more than the price paid for exports.

Many industries and services were affected by strikes and this caused problems between the trade unions and the government. People began to argue that the unions were too powerful and that their activities were harming the UK.

The 1970s was also a time of serious unrest in Northern Ireland. In 1972, the Northern Ireland Parliament was suspended and Northern Ireland was directly ruled by the UK government. Some 3,000 people lost their lives in the decades after 1969 in the violence in Northern Ireland.

You should be able to identify all 15 British inventions (on this and the previous page) and when they were invented. You also need to be able to identify the inventors.

MARY PETERS (1939–)

Born in Manchester, Mary Peters moved to Northern Ireland as a child. She was a talented athlete who won an Olympic gold medal in the pentathlon in 1972. After this, she raised money for local athletics and became the team manager for the women's British Olympic team. She continues to promote sport and tourism in Northern Ireland and was made a Dame of the British Empire in 2000 in recognition of her work.

EUROPE AND THE COMMON MARKET

West Germany, France, Belgium, Italy, Luxembourg and the Netherlands formed the European Economic Community (EEC) in 1957. At first the UK did not wish to join the EEC but it eventually did so in 1973. The UK is a full member of the European Union but does not use the Euro currency.

CONSERVATIVE GOVERNMENT FROM 1979 TO 1997

MARGARET THATCHER (1925–2013)

© Richard Baker/In Pictures/Corbis

Margaret Thatcher was the daughter of a grocer from Grantham in Lincolnshire. She trained as a chemist and lawyer. She was elected as a Conservative MP in 1959 and became a cabinet minister in 1970 as the Secretary of State for Education and Science. In 1975 she was elected as Leader of the Conservative Party and so became Leader of the Opposition.

Following the Conservative victory in the General Election in 1979, Margaret Thatcher became the first woman Prime Minister of the UK. She was the longest-serving Prime Minister of the 20th century, remaining in office until 1990.

During her premiership, there were a number of important economic reforms within the UK. She worked closely with the United States President, Ronald Reagan, and was one of the first Western leaders to recognise and welcome the changes in the leadership of the Soviet Union which eventually led to the end of the Cold War.

Margaret Thatcher, Britain's first woman Prime Minister, led the Conservative government from 1979 to 1990. The government made structural changes to the economy through the privatisation of nationalised industries and imposed legal controls on trade union powers. Deregulation saw a great increase in the role of the City of London as an international centre for investments, insurance and other financial services. Traditional industries, such as shipbuilding and coal mining, declined. In 1982, Argentina invaded the Falkland Islands, a British overseas territory in the South Atlantic. A naval taskforce was sent from the UK and military action led to the recovery of the islands.

John Major was Prime Minister after Mrs Thatcher, and helped establish the Northern Ireland peace process.

ROALD DAHL (1916–90)

Roald Dahl was born in Wales to Norwegian parents. He served in the Royal Air Force during the Second World War. It was during the 1940s that he began to publish books and short stories. He is most well known for his children's books, although he also wrote for adults. His best-known works include *Charlie and the Chocolate Factory* and *George's Marvellous Medicine*. Several of his books have been made into films.

LABOUR GOVERNMENT FROM 1997 TO 2010

In 1997 the Labour Party led by Tony Blair was elected. The Blair government introduced a Scottish Parliament and a Welsh Assembly (see page 115). The Scottish Parliament has substantial powers to legislate. The Welsh Assembly was given fewer legislative powers but considerable control over public services. In Northern Ireland, the Blair government was able to build on the peace process, resulting in the Good Friday Agreement signed in 1998. The Northern Ireland Assembly was elected in 1999 but suspended in 2002. It was not reinstated until 2007. Most paramilitary groups in Northern Ireland have decommissioned their arms and are inactive. Gordon Brown took over as Prime Minister in 2007.

> **66**
> In Northern Ireland, the Blair government was able to build on the peace process, resulting in the Good Friday Agreement signed in 1998.
> **99**

CONFLICTS IN AFGHANISTAN AND IRAQ

Throughout the 1990s, Britain played a leading role in coalition forces involved in the liberation of Kuwait, following the Iraqi invasion in 1990, and the conflict in the Former Republic of Yugoslavia. Since 2000, British armed forces have been engaged in the global fight against international terrorism and against the proliferation of weapons of mass destruction, including operations in Afghanistan and Iraq. British combat troops left Iraq in 2009. The UK now operates in Afghanistan as part of the United Nations (UN) mandated 50-nation International Security Assistance Force

> In May 2010, and for the first time in the UK since February 1974, no political party won an overall majority in the General Election.

(ISAF) coalition and at the invitation of the Afghan government. ISAF is working to ensure that Afghan territory can never again be used as a safe haven for international terrorism, where groups such as Al Qa'ida could plan attacks on the international community. As part of this, ISAF is building up the Afghan National Security Forces and is helping to create a secure environment in which governance and development can be extended. International forces are gradually handing over responsibility for security to the Afghans, who will have full security responsibility in all provinces by the end of 2014.

COALITION GOVERNMENT 2010 ONWARDS

In May 2010, and for the first time in the UK since February 1974, no political party won an overall majority in the General Election. The Conservative and Liberal Democrat parties formed a coalition and the leader of the Conservative Party, David Cameron, became Prime Minister.

Check that you understand:

- The establishment of the welfare state

- How life in Britain changed in the 1960s and 1970s

- British inventions of the 20th century (you do not need to remember dates of births and deaths)

- Events since 1979

CHAPTER 5
A modern, thriving society

> **→ IN THIS CHAPTER** you will learn about the population and culture of the UK. The start of the chapter shows you where the major cities of the UK are. You should be sure you can identify the various cities, such as Leeds and Bradford, confidently. Because the UK is a multicultural country you will also have to know the sizes of the different ethnic and religious groups in the UK, as well as their main festivals.

The chapter focuses on British culture after that and you should make sure you know who each of the people described are and what they have achieved. Britain's recent sporting success at the Olympics features heavily so focus on who won medals and for what as well as the general information about sport in the UK. Make sure you familiarise yourself with the poems, films, books and other works listed too, as well as the artists, composers, architects, authors, poets and other famous people. You should also familiarise yourself with the extracts of poems provided and be able to recognise the famous landmarks at the end of the chapter.

IN THIS CHAPTER THERE IS INFORMATION ABOUT:

- The cities and population of the UK
- Religious festivals of the UK
- Popular sports and famous sportsmen and women
- The development of music, including famous composers
- British theatre and cinema through the ages
- British artists and architects
- Famous British poets and authors
- Sections of famous British poems
- British comedy and leisure activities
- Famous British landmarks

The UK today

> Post-war immigration means that nearly 10% of the population has a parent or grandparent born outside the UK.

The UK today is a more diverse society than it was 100 years ago, in both ethnic and religious terms. Post-war immigration means that nearly 10% of the population has a parent or grandparent born outside the UK. The UK continues to be a multinational and multiracial society with a rich and varied culture. This section will tell you about the different parts of the UK and some of the important places. It will also explain some of the UK's traditions and customs and some of the popular activities that take place.

THE NATIONS OF THE UK

The UK is located in the north west of Europe. The longest distance on the mainland is from John O'Groats on the north coast of Scotland to Land's End in the south-west corner of England. It is about 870 miles (approximately 1,400 kilometres).

Most people live in towns and cities but much of Britain is still countryside. Many people continue to visit the countryside for holidays and for leisure activities such as walking, camping and fishing.

CITIES OF THE UK

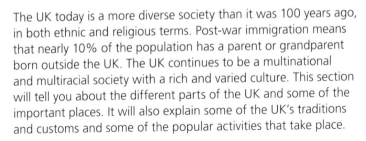

ENGLAND

1	London
2	Birmingham
3	Liverpool
4	Leeds
5	Sheffield
6	Bristol
7	Manchester
8	Bradford
9	Newcastle Upon Tyne
10	Plymouth
11	Southampton
12	Norwich

WALES

13	Cardiff
14	Swansea
15	Newport

NORTHERN IRELAND

16	Belfast

SCOTLAND

17	Edinburgh
18	Glasgow
19	Dundee
20	Aberdeen

CAPITAL CITIES

The capital city of the UK is London

Scotland
The capital city of
Scotland is Edinburgh

Wales
The capital city of Wales
is Cardiff

Northern Ireland
The capital city of
Northern Ireland is Belfast

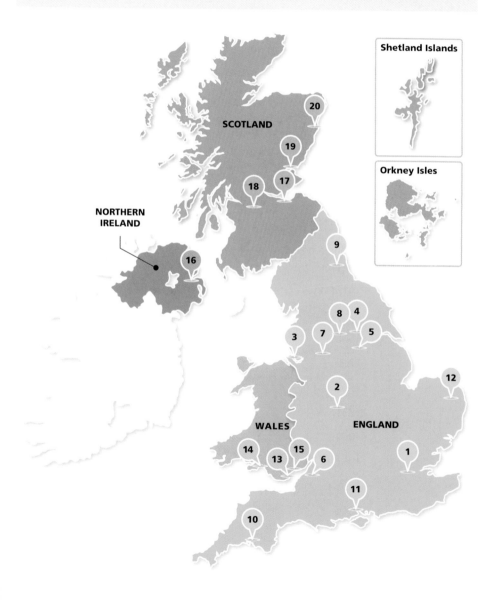

UK CURRENCY

The currency in the UK is the pound sterling (symbol £). There are 100 pence in a pound. The denominations (values) of currency are:

coins: 1p, 2p, 5p, 10p, 20p, 50p, £1 and £2

notes: £5, £10, £20, £50.

Northern Ireland and Scotland have their own banknotes, which are valid everywhere in the UK. However, shops and businesses do not have to accept them.

LANGUAGES AND DIALECTS

There are many variations in language in the different parts of the UK. The English language has many accents and dialects. In Wales, many people speak Welsh – a completely different language from English – and it is taught in schools and universities. In Scotland, Gaelic (again, a different language) is spoken in some parts of the Highlands and Islands, and in Northern Ireland some people speak Irish Gaelic.

> In Scotland, Gaelic is spoken in some parts of the Highlands and Islands, and in Northern Ireland some people speak Irish Gaelic.

POPULATION

The table below shows how the population of the UK has changed over time.

Population growth in the UK

Year	Population
1600	Just over 4 million
1700	5 million
1801	8 million
1851	20 million
1901	40 million
1951	50 million
1998	57 million
2005	Just under 60 million
2010	Just over 62 million

Source: National Statistics

Population growth has been faster in more recent years. Migration into the UK and longer life expectancy have played a part in population growth.

The population is very unequally distributed over the four parts of the UK. England more or less consistently makes up 84% of the total population, Wales around 5%, Scotland just over 8% and Northern Ireland less than 3%.

Population distribution across the UK

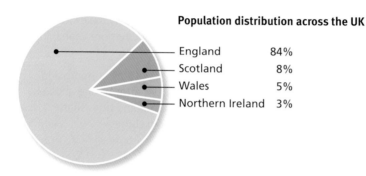

England	84%
Scotland	8%
Wales	5%
Northern Ireland	3%

> Within the UK, it is a legal requirement that men and women should not be discriminated against because of their gender or because they are, or are not, married.

AN AGEING POPULATION

People in the UK are living longer than ever before. This is due to improved living standards and better health care. There are now a record number of people aged 85 and over. This has an impact on the cost of pensions and health care.

ETHNIC DIVERSITY

The UK population is ethnically diverse and changing rapidly, especially in large cities such as London. It is not always easy to get an exact picture of the ethnic origin of all the population.

There are people in the UK with ethnic origins from all over the world. In surveys, the most common ethnic description chosen is white, which includes people of European, Australian, Canadian, New Zealand and American descent. Other significant groups are those of Asian, black and mixed descent.

AN EQUAL SOCIETY

Within the UK, it is a legal requirement that men and women should not be discriminated against because of their gender or because they are, or are not, married. They have equal rights to work, own property, marry and divorce. If they are married, both parents are equally responsible for their children.

Women in Britain today make up about half of the workforce. On average, girls leave school with better qualifications than boys. More women than men study at university.

Employment opportunities for women are much greater than they were in the past. Women work in all sectors of the economy, and there are now more women in high-level positions than ever before, including senior managers in traditionally male-dominated occupations. Alongside this, men now work in more varied jobs than they did in the past.

It is no longer expected that women should stay at home and not work. Women often continue to work after having children. In many families today, both partners work and both share responsibility for childcare and household chores.

Check that you understand:

• The capital cities of the UK

• What languages other than English are spoken in particular parts of the UK

• How the population of the UK has changed

• That the UK is an equal society and ethnically diverse

• The currency of the UK

Religion

The UK is historically a Christian country. In the 2009 Citizenship Survey, 70% of people identified themselves as Christian. Much smaller proportions identified themselves as Muslim (4%), Hindu (2%), Sikh (1%), Jewish or Buddhist (both less than 0.5%), and 2% of people followed another religion. There are religious buildings for other religions all over the UK. This includes Islamic mosques, Hindu temples, Jewish synagogues, Sikh gurdwaras and Buddhist temples. However, everyone has the legal right to choose their religion, or to choose not to practise a religion. In the Citizenship Survey, 21% of people said that they had no religion.

Religions of the UK

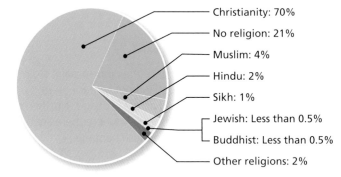

Christianity: 70%

No religion: 21%

Muslim: 4%

Hindu: 2%

Sikh: 1%

Jewish: Less than 0.5%

Buddhist: Less than 0.5%

Other religions: 2%

CHRISTIAN CHURCHES

In England, there is a constitutional link between Church and state. The official Church of the state is the Church of England (called the Anglican Church in other countries and the Episcopal Church in Scotland and the United States). It is a Protestant Church and has existed since the Reformation in the 1530s (see pages 22–4 for an explanation).

The monarch is the head of the Church of England. The spiritual leader of the Church of England is the Archbishop of Canterbury. The monarch has the right to select the Archbishop and other senior church officials, but usually the choice is made by the Prime Minister and a committee appointed by the Church. Several Church of England bishops sit in the House of Lords (see page 111).

In Scotland, the national Church is the Church of Scotland, which is a Presbyterian Church. It is governed by ministers and elders. The chairperson of the General Assembly of the Church of Scotland is the Moderator, who is appointed for one year only and often speaks on behalf of that Church.

There is no established Church in Wales or Northern Ireland.

Other Protestant Christian groups in the UK are Baptists, Methodists, Presbyterians and Quakers. There are also other denominations of Christianity, the biggest of which is Roman Catholic.

> The monarch has the right to select the Archbishop and other senior church officials, but usually the choice is made by the Prime Minister and a committee appointed by the Church.

PATRON SAINTS' DAYS

England, Scotland, Wales and Northern Ireland each have a national saint, called a patron saint. Each saint has a special day:

- 1 March: St David's Day, Wales
- 17 March: St Patrick's Day, Northern Ireland
- 23 April: St George's Day, England
- 30 November: St Andrew's Day, Scotland.

Only Scotland and Northern Ireland have their patron saint's day as an official holiday (although in Scotland not all businesses and offices will close). Events are held across Scotland, Northern Ireland and the rest of the country, especially where there are a lot of people of Scottish, Northern Irish and Irish heritage.

While the patron saints' days are no longer public holidays in England and Wales, they are still celebrated. Parades and small festivals are held all over the two countries.

Westminster Abbey has been the coronation church since 1066 and is the final resting place of 17 monarchs

Check that you understand:

- The different religions that are practised in the UK

- That the Anglican Church, also known as the Church of England, is the Church of the state in England (the 'established Church')

- That other branches of the Christian Church also practise their faith in the UK without being linked to the state

- That other religions are practised in the UK

- About the patron saints

Customs and traditions

THE MAIN CHRISTIAN FESTIVALS

Christmas Day, 25 December, celebrates the birth of Jesus Christ. It is a public holiday. Many Christians go to church on Christmas Eve (24 December) or on Christmas Day itself.

Christmas is celebrated in a traditional way. People usually spend the day at home and eat a special meal, which often includes roast turkey, Christmas pudding and mince pies. They give gifts, send cards and decorate their houses. Christmas is a special time for children. Very young children believe that Father Christmas (also known as Santa Claus) brings them presents during the night before Christmas Day. Many people decorate a tree in their home.

A typical Christmas Day meal

Boxing Day is the day after Christmas Day and is a public holiday.

> The 40 days before Easter are known as Lent. It is a time when Christians take time to reflect and prepare for Easter.

Easter takes place in March or April. It marks the death of Jesus Christ on Good Friday and his rising from the dead on Easter Sunday. Both Good Friday and the following Monday, called Easter Monday, are public holidays.

The 40 days before Easter are known as Lent. It is a time when Christians take time to reflect and prepare for Easter. Traditionally, people would fast during this period and today many people will give something up, like a favourite food. The day before Lent starts is called Shrove Tuesday, or Pancake Day. People eat pancakes, which were traditionally made to use up foods such as eggs, fat and milk before fasting. Lent begins on Ash Wednesday. There are church services where Christians are marked with an ash cross on their forehead as a symbol of death and sorrow for sin.

Easter is also celebrated by people who are not religious. 'Easter eggs' are chocolate eggs often given as presents at Easter as a symbol of new life.

OTHER RELIGIOUS FESTIVALS

Diwali normally falls in October or November and lasts for five days. It is often called the Festival of Lights. It is celebrated by Hindus and Sikhs. It celebrates the victory of good over evil and the gaining of knowledge. There are different stories about how the festival came about. There is a famous celebration of Diwali in Leicester.

Diwali is popularly known as the Festival of Lights

Hannukah is in November or December and is celebrated for eight days. It is to remember the Jews' struggle for religious freedom. On each day of the festival a candle is lit on a stand of eight candles (called a menorah) to remember the story of the festival, where oil that should have lasted only a day did so for eight.

Eid al-Fitr celebrates the end of Ramadan, when Muslims have fasted for a month. They thank Allah for giving them the strength to complete the fast. The date when it takes place changes every year. Muslims attend special services and meals.

Eid ul Adha remembers that the prophet Ibrahim was willing to sacrifice his son when God ordered him to. It reminds Muslims of their own commitment to God. Many Muslims sacrifice an animal to eat during this festival. In Britain this has to be done in a slaughterhouse.

Vaisakhi (also spelled Baisakhi) is a Sikh festival which celebrates the founding of the Sikh community known as the Khalsa. It is celebrated on 14 April each year with parades, dancing and singing.

The menorah used during Hannukah typically has 9 candles. The middle candle remains lit throughout the festival and is used to light the other 8. However, for the purposes of your test you should learn the material as reproduced here.

OTHER FESTIVALS AND TRADITIONS

New Year, 1 January, is a public holiday. People usually celebrate on the night of 31 December (called New Year's Eve). In Scotland, 31 December is called Hogmanay and 2 January is also a public holiday. For some Scottish people, Hogmanay is a bigger holiday than Christmas.

Valentine's Day, 14 February, is when lovers exchange cards and gifts. Sometimes people send anonymous cards to someone they secretly admire.

April Fool's Day, 1 April, is a day when people play jokes on each other until midday. The television and newspapers often have stories that are April Fool jokes.

Mothering Sunday (or Mother's Day) is the Sunday three weeks before Easter. Children send cards or buy gifts for their mothers.

Father's Day is the third Sunday in June. Children send cards or buy gifts for their fathers.

Halloween, 31 October, is an ancient festival and has roots in the pagan festival to mark the beginning of winter. Young people will often dress up in frightening costumes to play 'trick or treat'. People give them treats to stop them playing tricks on them. A lot of people carve lanterns out of pumpkins and put a candle inside.

Bonfire Night, 5 November, is an occasion when people in Great Britain set off fireworks at home or in special displays. The origin of this celebration was an event in 1605, when a group of Catholics led by Guy Fawkes failed in their plan to kill the Protestant king with a bomb in the Houses of Parliament.

Remembrance Day, 11 November, commemorates those who died fighting for the UK and its allies. Originally it commemorated the dead of the First World War, which ended on 11 November 1918. People wear poppies (the red flower found on the battlefields of the First World War). At 11.00 am there is a two-minute silence and wreaths are laid at the Cenotaph in Whitehall, London.

You need to know the dates of key festivals and traditions. Take some time to learn what is associated with each event as well, such as special foods or traditions.

Unveiled in 1920, the Cenotaph is the centrepiece to the Remembrance Day service

BANK HOLIDAYS

As well as those mentioned previously, there are other public holidays each year called bank holidays, when banks and many other businesses are closed for the day. These are of no religious significance. They are at the beginning of May, in late May or early June, and in August. In Northern Ireland, the anniversary of the Battle of the Boyne in July is also a public holiday.

Check that you understand:

- The main Christian festivals that are celebrated in the UK
- Other religious festivals that are important in the UK
- Some of the other events that are celebrated in the UK
- What a bank holiday is

Sport

Sports of all kinds play an important part in many people's lives. There are several sports that are particularly popular in the UK. Many sporting events take place at major stadiums such as Wembley Stadium in London and the Millennium Stadium in Cardiff.

Local governments and private companies provide sports facilities such as swimming pools, tennis courts, football pitches, dry ski slopes and gymnasiums. Many famous sports, including cricket, football, lawn tennis, golf and rugby, began in Britain.

The UK has hosted the Olympic Games on three occasions: 1908, 1948 and 2012. The main Olympic site for the 2012 Games was in Stratford, East London. The British team was very successful, across a wide range of Olympic sports, finishing third in the medal table.

The Paralympic Games for 2012 were also hosted in London. The Paralympics have their origin in the work of Dr Sir Ludwig Guttman, a German refugee, at the Stoke Mandeville hospital in Buckinghamshire. Dr Guttman developed new methods of treatment for people with spinal injuries and encouraged patients to take part in exercise and sport.

> " The UK has hosted the Olympic Games on three occasions: 1908, 1948 and 2012. "

NOTABLE BRITISH SPORTSMEN AND WOMEN

Sir Roger Bannister (1929–) was the first man in the world to run a mile in under four minutes, in 1954.

Sir Jackie Stewart (1939–) is a Scottish former racing driver who won the Formula 1 world championship three times.

Bobby Moore (1941–93) captained the English football team that won the World Cup in 1966.

Sir Ian Botham (1955–) captained the English cricket team and holds a number of English Test cricket records, both for batting and for bowling.

Jayne Torvill (1957–) and **Christopher Dean (1958–)** won gold medals for ice dancing at the Olympic Games in 1984 and in four consecutive world championships.

Sir Steve Redgrave (1962–) won gold medals in rowing in five consecutive Olympic Games and is one of Britain's greatest Olympians.

Baroness Tanni-Grey Thompson (1969–) is an athlete who uses a wheelchair and won 16 Paralympic medals, including 11 gold medals, in races over five Paralympic Games. She won the London Marathon six times and broke a total of 30 world records.

Dame Kelly Holmes (1970–) won two gold medals for running in the 2004 Olympic Games. She has held a number of British and European records.

Dame Ellen MacArthur (1976–) is a yachtswoman and in 2004 became the fastest person to sail around the world single-handed.

Sir Chris Hoy (1976–) is a Scottish cyclist who has won six gold and one silver Olympic medals. He has also won 11 world championship titles.

David Weir (1979–) is a Paralympian who uses a wheelchair and has won six gold medals over two Paralympic Games. He has also won the London Marathon six times.

Bradley Wiggins (1980–) is a cyclist. In 2012, he became the first Briton to win the Tour de France. He has won seven Olympic medals, including gold medals in the 2004, 2008 and 2012 Olympic Games.

Mo Farah (1983–) is a British distance runner, born in Somalia. He won gold medals in the 2012 Olympics for the 5,000 and 10,000 metres and is the first Briton to win the Olympic gold medal in the 10,000 metres.

Jessica Ennis (1986–) is an athlete. She won the 2012 Olympic gold medal in the heptathlon, which includes seven different track and field events. She also holds a number of British athletics records.

Andy Murray (1987–) is a Scottish tennis player who in 2012 won the men's singles in the US Open. He is the first British man to win a singles title in a Grand Slam tournament since 1936. In the same year, he won Olympic gold and silver medals and was runner-up in the men's singles at Wimbledon (see page 78).

Ellie Simmonds (1994–) is a Paralympian who won gold medals for swimming at the 2008 and 2012 Paralympic Games and holds a number of world records. She was the youngest member of the British team at the 2008 Games.

Make sure you are familiar with this list of sportsmen and women, including which sports they are famous for and any medals or records they won.

CRICKET

Cricket originated in England and is now played in many countries. Games can last up to five days but still result in a draw! The idiosyncratic nature of the game and its complex laws are said to reflect the best of the British character and sense of fair play. You may come across expressions such as 'rain stopped play', 'batting on a sticky wicket', 'playing a straight bat', 'bowled a googly' or 'it's just not cricket', which have passed into everyday usage. The most famous competition is the Ashes, which is a series of Test matches played between England and Australia.

Cricket is one of the many famous sports originating in Britain

© Adrian Murrell/Getty Images

FOOTBALL

Football is the UK's most popular sport. It has a long history in the UK and the first professional football clubs were formed in the late 19th century.

England, Scotland, Wales and Northern Ireland each have separate leagues in which clubs representing different towns and cities compete. The English Premier League attracts a huge international audience. Many of the best players in the world play in the Premier League. Many UK teams also compete in competitions such as the UEFA (Union of European Football Associations) Champions League, against other teams from Europe. Most towns and cities have a professional club and people take great pride in supporting their home team. There can be great rivalry between different football clubs and among fans.

Each country in the UK also has its own national team that competes with other national teams across the world in tournaments such as the FIFA (Fédération Internationale de Football Association) World Cup and the UEFA European Football Championships. England's only international tournament victory was at the World Cup of 1966, hosted in the UK.

Football is also a popular sport to play in many local communities, with people playing amateur games every week in parks all over the UK.

RUGBY

Rugby originated in England in the early 19th century and is very popular in the UK today. There are two different types of rugby, which have different rules: union and league. Both have separate leagues and national teams in England, Wales, Scotland and Northern Ireland (who play with the Irish Republic). Teams from all countries compete in a range of competitions. The most famous rugby union competition is the Six Nations Championship between England, Ireland, Scotland, Wales, France and Italy. The Super League is the most well-known rugby league (club) competition.

HORSE RACING

There is a very long history of horse racing in Britain, with evidence of events taking place as far back as Roman times. The sport has a long association with royalty. There are racecourses all over the UK. Famous horse-racing events include: Royal Ascot, a five-day race meeting in Berkshire attended by members of the Royal Family; the Grand National at Aintree near Liverpool; and the Scottish Grand National at Ayr. There is a National Horseracing Museum in Newmarket, Suffolk.

GOLF

The modern game of golf can be traced back to 15th-century Scotland. It is a popular sport played socially as well as professionally. There are public and private golf courses all over the UK. St Andrews in Scotland is known as the home of golf. The Open Championship is the only 'Major' tournament held outside the United States. It is hosted by a different golf course every year.

> There are two different types of rugby, which have different rules: union and league. Both have separate leagues and national teams in England, Wales, Scotland and Northern Ireland (who play with the Irish Republic).

TENNIS

Modern tennis evolved in England in the late 19th century. The first tennis club was founded in Leamington Spa in 1872. The most famous tournament hosted in Britain is The Wimbledon Championships, which takes place each year at the All England Lawn Tennis and Croquet Club. It is the oldest tennis tournament in the world and the only 'Grand Slam' event played on grass.

WATER SPORTS

Sailing continues to be popular in the UK, reflecting our maritime heritage. A British sailor, Sir Francis Chichester, was the first person to sail single-handed around the world, in 1966/67. Two years later, Sir Robin Knox-Johnston became the first person to do this without stopping. Many sailing events are held throughout the UK, the most famous of which is at Cowes on the Isle of Wight.

Rowing is also popular, both as a leisure activity and as a competitive sport. There is a popular yearly race on the Thames between Oxford and Cambridge Universities.

A British sailor, Sir Francis Chichester, was the first person to sail single-handed around the world, in 1966/67. Two years later, Sir Robin Knox-Johnston became the first person to do this without stopping.

MOTOR SPORTS

There is a long history of motor sport in the UK, for both cars and motor cycles. Motor-car racing in the UK started in 1902. The UK continues to be a world leader in the development and manufacture of motor-sport technology. A Formula 1 Grand Prix event is held in the UK each year and a number of British Grand Prix drivers have won the Formula 1 World Championship. Recent British winners include Damon Hill, Lewis Hamilton and Jenson Button.

SKIING

Skiing is increasingly popular in the UK. Many people go abroad to ski and there are also dry ski slopes throughout the UK. Skiing on snow may also be possible during the winter. There are five ski centres in Scotland, as well as Europe's longest dry ski slope near Edinburgh.

Arts and culture

MUSIC

Music is an important part of British culture, with a rich and varied heritage. It ranges from classical music to modern pop. There are many different venues and musical events that take place across the UK.

The Proms is an eight-week summer season of orchestral classical music that takes place in various venues, including the Royal Albert Hall in London. It has been organised by the British Broadcasting Corporation (BBC) since 1927. The Last Night of the Proms is the most well-known concert and (along with others in the series) is broadcast on television.

Classical music has been popular in the UK for many centuries. **Henry Purcell (1659–95)** was the organist at Westminster Abbey. He wrote church music, operas and other pieces, and developed a British style distinct from that elsewhere in Europe. He continues to be influential on British composers.

The German-born composer **George Frederick Handel (1685– 1759)** spent many years in the UK and became a British citizen in 1727. He wrote the *Water Music* for King George I and *Music for the Royal Fireworks* for his son, George II. Both these pieces continue to be very popular. Handel also wrote an oratorio, *Messiah*, which is sung regularly by choirs, often at Easter time.

More recently, important composers include **Gustav Holst (1874– 1934)**, whose work includes *The Planets*, a suite of pieces themed around the planets of the solar system. He adapted *Jupiter*, part of the *Planets* suite, as the tune for *I vow to thee my country*, a popular hymn in British churches.

Sir Edward Elgar (1857–1934) was born in Worcester, England. His best-known work is probably the *Pomp and Circumstance Marches*. *March No 1 (Land of Hope and Glory)* is usually played at the Last Night of the Proms at the Royal Albert Hall.

Ralph Vaughan Williams (1872–1958) wrote music for orchestras and choirs. He was strongly influenced by traditional English folk music.

The German-born composer George Frederick Handel (1685– 1759) spent many years in the UK and became a British citizen in 1727.

The Royal Albert Hall is the venue for the Last Night of the Proms

© Adam Woolfitt/Corbis

?

You should be familiar with the lives and works of these famous composers (here and on the previous page). This includes details such as Handel being born in Germany.

Sir William Walton (1902–83) wrote a wide range of music, from film scores to opera. He wrote marches for the coronations of King George VI and Queen Elizabeth II but his best-known works are probably *Façade*, which became a ballet, and *Belshazzar's Feast*, which is intended to be sung by a large choir.

Benjamin Britten (1913–76) is best known for his operas, which include *Peter Grimes* and *Billy Budd*. He also wrote *A Young Person's Guide to the Orchestra*, which is based on a piece of music by Purcell and introduces the listener to the various different sections of an orchestra. He founded the Aldeburgh festival in Suffolk, which continues to be a popular music event of international importance.

Other types of popular music, including folk music, jazz, pop and rock music, have flourished in Britain since the 20th century. Britain has had an impact on popular music around the world, due to the wide use of the English language, the UK's cultural links with many countries, and British capacity for invention and innovation.

Since the 1960s, British pop music has made one of the most important cultural contributions to life in the UK. Bands including The Beatles and The Rolling Stones continue to have an influence on music both here and abroad. British pop music has continued to innovate – for example, the Punk movement of the late 1970s, and the trend towards boy and girl bands in the 1990s.

There are many large venues that host music events throughout the year, such as: Wembley Stadium; The O2 in Greenwich, south-east London; and the Scottish Exhibition and Conference Centre (SECC) in Glasgow.

Festival season takes place across the UK every summer, with major events in various locations. Famous festivals include Glastonbury, the Isle of Wight Festival and the V Festival. Many bands and solo artists, both well-known and up-and-coming, perform at these events.

The National Eisteddfod of Wales is an annual cultural festival which includes music, dance, art and original performances largely in Welsh. It includes a number of important competitions for Welsh poetry.

The Mercury Music Prize is awarded each September for the best album from the UK and Ireland. The Brit Awards is an annual event that gives awards in a range of categories, such as best British group and best British solo artist.

THEATRE

There are theatres in most towns and cities throughout the UK, ranging from the large to the small. They are an important part of local communities and often show both professional and amateur productions. London's West End, also known as 'Theatreland', is particularly well known. *The Mousetrap*, a murder-mystery play by Dame Agatha Christie, has been running in the West End since 1952 and has had the longest initial run of any show in history.

> **The National Eisteddfod of Wales is an annual cultural festival which includes music, dance, art and original performances largely in Welsh.**

There is also a strong tradition of musical theatre in the UK. In the 19th century, Gilbert and Sullivan wrote comic operas, often making fun of popular culture and politics. These operas include *HMS Pinafore*, *The Pirates of Penzance* and *The Mikado*. Gilbert and Sullivan's work is still often staged by professional and amateur groups. More recently, Andrew Lloyd Webber has written the music for shows which have been popular throughout the world, including, in collaboration with Tim Rice, *Jesus Christ Superstar* and *Evita*, and also *Cats* and *The Phantom of the Opera*.

One British tradition is the pantomime. Many theatres produce a pantomime at Christmas time. They are based on fairy stories and are light-hearted plays with music and comedy, enjoyed by family audiences. One of the traditional characters is the Dame, a woman played by a man. There is often also a pantomime horse or cow played by two actors in the same costume.

The Edinburgh Festival takes place in Edinburgh, Scotland, every summer. It is a series of different arts and cultural festivals, with the biggest and most well-known being the Edinburgh Festival Fringe ('the Fringe'). The Fringe is a showcase of mainly theatre and comedy performances. It often shows experimental work.

The Laurence Olivier Awards take place annually at different venues in London. There are a variety of categories, including best director, best actor and best actress. The awards are named after the British actor Sir Laurence Olivier, later Lord Olivier, who was best known for his roles in various Shakespeare plays.

ART

During the Middle Ages, most art had a religious theme, particularly wall paintings in churches and illustrations in religious books. Much of this was lost after the Protestant Reformation but wealthy families began to collect other paintings and sculptures. Many of the painters working in Britain in the 16th and 17th centuries were from abroad – for example, Hans Holbein and Sir Anthony Van Dyck. British artists, particularly those painting portraits and landscapes, became well known from the 18th century onwards.

Works by British and international artists are displayed in galleries across the UK. Some of the most well-known galleries are The National Gallery, Tate Britain and Tate Modern in London, the National Museum in Cardiff, and the National Gallery of Scotland in Edinburgh.

Tate Modern is based in the former Bankside Power Station in central London

The Turner Prize was established in 1984 and celebrates contemporary art. It was named after Joseph Turner. Four works are shortlisted every year and shown at Tate Britain before the winner is announced. The Turner Prize is recognised as one of the most prestigious visual art awards in Europe. Previous winners include Damien Hirst and Richard Wright.

NOTABLE BRITISH ARTISTS

Thomas Gainsborough (1727–88) was a portrait painter who often painted people in country or garden scenery.

David Allan (1744–96) was a Scottish painter who was best known for painting portraits. One of his most famous works is called *The Origin of Painting*.

Joseph Turner (1775–1851) was an influential landscape painter in a modern style. He is considered the artist who raised the profile of landscape painting.

John Constable (1776–1837) was a landscape painter most famous for his works of Dedham Vale on the Suffolk–Essex border in the east of England.

The Pre-Raphaelites were an important group of artists in the second half of the 19th century. They painted detailed pictures on religious or literary themes in bright colours. The group included Holman Hunt, Dante Gabriel Rossetti and Sir John Millais.

Sir John Lavery (1856–1941) was a very successful Northern Irish portrait painter. His work included painting the Royal Family.

Henry Moore (1898–1986) was an English sculptor and artist. He is best known for his large bronze abstract sculptures.

John Petts (1914–91) was a Welsh artist, best known for his engravings and stained glass.

Lucian Freud (1922–2011) was a German-born British artist. He is best known for his portraits.

David Hockney (1937–) was an important contributor to the 'pop art' movement of the 1960s and continues to be influential today.

> **?**
>
> You may be asked questions about these artists and their work. Make sure you know about trends in British art as well, such as the development of landscape painting.

ARCHITECTURE

The architectural heritage of the UK is rich and varied. In the Middle Ages, great cathedrals and churches were built, many of which still stand today. Examples are the cathedrals in Durham, Lincoln, Canterbury and Salisbury. The White Tower in the Tower of London is an example of a Norman castle keep, built on the orders of William the Conqueror (see pages 15–6 and 102).

Gradually, as the countryside became more peaceful and landowners became richer, the houses of the wealthy became more elaborate and great country houses such as Hardwick Hall in Derbyshire were built. British styles of architecture began to evolve.

> In the 17th century, Inigo Jones took inspiration from classical architecture to design the Queen's House at Greenwich and the Banqueting House in Whitehall in London.

In the 17th century, Inigo Jones took inspiration from classical architecture to design the Queen's House at Greenwich and the Banqueting House in Whitehall in London. Later in the century, Sir Christopher Wren helped develop a British version of the ornate styles popular in Europe in buildings such as the new St Paul's Cathedral.

In the 18th century, simpler designs became popular. The Scottish architect Robert Adam influenced the development of architecture in the UK, Europe and America. He designed the inside decoration as well as the building itself in great houses such as Dumfries House in Scotland. His ideas influenced architects in cities such as Bath, where the Royal Crescent was built.

In the 19th century, the medieval 'gothic' style became popular again. As cities expanded, many great public buildings were built in this style. The Houses of Parliament and St Pancras Station were built at this time, as were the town halls in cities such as Manchester and Sheffield.

In the 20th century, Sir Edwin Lutyens had an influence throughout the British Empire. He designed New Delhi to be the seat of government in India. After the First World War, he was responsible for many war memorials throughout the world, including the Cenotaph in Whitehall. The Cenotaph is the site of the annual Remembrance Day service attended by the Queen, politicians and foreign ambassadors (see pages 72–3).

Modern British architects including Sir Norman Foster, Lord (Richard) Rogers and Dame Zaha Hadid continue to work on major projects throughout the world as well as within the UK.

Alongside the development of architecture, garden design and landscaping have played an important role in the UK. In the 18th century, Lancelot 'Capability' Brown designed the grounds around country houses so that the landscape appeared to be natural, with grass, trees and lakes. He often said that a place had 'capabilities'. Later, Gertrude Jekyll often worked with Edwin Lutyens to design colourful gardens around the houses he designed. Gardens continue to be an important part of homes in the UK. The annual Chelsea Flower Show showcases garden design from Britain and around the world.

FASHION AND DESIGN

Britain has produced many great designers, from Thomas Chippendale (who designed furniture in the 18th century) to Clarice Cliff (who designed Art Deco ceramics) to Sir Terence Conran (a 20th-century interior designer). Leading fashion designers of recent years include Mary Quant, Alexander McQueen and Vivienne Westwood.

LITERATURE

The UK has a prestigious literary history and tradition. Several British writers, including the novelist Sir William Golding, the poet Seamus Heaney, and the playwright Harold Pinter, have won the Nobel Prize in Literature. Other authors have become well known in popular fiction. Agatha Christie's detective stories are read all over the world and Ian Fleming's books introduced James Bond. In 2003, *The Lord of the Rings* by JRR Tolkien was voted the country's best-loved novel.

The Man Booker Prize for Fiction is awarded annually for the best fiction novel written by an author from the Commonwealth, Ireland or Zimbabwe. It has been awarded since 1968. Past winners include Ian McEwan, Hilary Mantel and Julian Barnes.

Since 2014 the Man Booker Prize is awarded for fiction novels originally written in English and published in the UK by authors from anywhere in the world. However, for the purposes of your test you must learn the material as reproduced here.

NOTABLE AUTHORS AND WRITERS

Jane Austen (1775–1817) was an English novelist. Her books include *Pride and Prejudice* and *Sense and Sensibility.* Her novels are concerned with marriage and family relationships. Many have been made into television programmes or films.

Charles Dickens (1812–70) wrote a number of very famous novels, including *Oliver Twist* and *Great Expectations.* You will hear references in everyday talk to some of the characters in his books, such as Scrooge (a mean person) or Mr Micawber (always hopeful).

Robert Louis Stevenson (1850–94) wrote books which are still read by adults and children today. His most famous books include *Treasure Island, Kidnapped* and *Dr Jekyll and Mr Hyde.*

Thomas Hardy (1840–1928) was an author and poet. His best-known novels focus on rural society and include *Far from the Madding Crowd* and *Jude the Obscure.*

Sir Arthur Conan Doyle (1859–1930) was a Scottish doctor and writer. He was best known for his stories about Sherlock Holmes, who was one of the first fictional detectives.

Evelyn Waugh (1903–66) wrote satirical novels, including *Decline and Fall* and *Scoop.* He is perhaps best known for *Brideshead Revisited.*

Sir Kingsley Amis (1922–95) was an English novelist and poet. He wrote more than 20 novels. The most well-known is *Lucky Jim.*

Graham Greene (1904–91) wrote novels often influenced by his religious beliefs, including *The Heart of the Matter, The Honorary Consul, Brighton Rock* and *Our Man in Havana.*

J K Rowling (1965–) wrote the Harry Potter series of children's books, which have enjoyed huge international success. She now writes fiction for adults as well.

You may be asked to identify famous British authors and poets, as well as famous books and poems. Make sure you know British winners of the Nobel Prize in Literature as well.

BRITISH POETS

British poetry is among the richest in the world. The Anglo-Saxon poem *Beowulf* tells of its hero's battles against monsters and is still translated into modern English. Poems which survive from the

Middle Ages include Chaucer's *Canterbury Tales* and a poem called *Sir Gawain and the Green Knight*, about one of the knights at the court of King Arthur.

As well as plays, Shakespeare wrote many sonnets (poems which must be 14 lines long) and some longer poems. As Protestant ideas spread, a number of poets wrote poems inspired by their religious views. One of these was John Milton, who wrote *Paradise Lost*.

Other poets, including William Wordsworth, were inspired by nature. Sir Walter Scott wrote poems inspired by Scotland and the traditional stories and songs from the area on the borders of Scotland and England. He also wrote novels, many of which were set in Scotland.

Poetry was very popular in the 19th century, with poets such as William Blake, John Keats, Lord Byron, Percy Shelley, Alfred Lord Tennyson, and Robert and Elizabeth Browning. Later, many poets – for example, Wilfred Owen and Siegfried Sassoon – were inspired to write about their experiences in the First World War. More recently, popular poets have included Sir Walter de la Mare, John Masefield, Sir John Betjeman and Ted Hughes.

Some of the best-known poets are buried or commemorated in Poet's Corner in Westminster Abbey.

Some famous lines include:

Poetry was very popular in the 19th century, with poets such as William Blake, John Keats, Lord Byron, Percy Shelley, Alfred Lord Tennyson, and Robert and Elizabeth Browning.

'Oh to be in England now that April's there
And whoever wakes in England sees, some morning, unaware,
That the lowest boughs and the brushwood sheaf
Round the elm-tree bole are in tiny leaf
While the Chaffinch sings on the orchard bough
In England – Now!'
(Robert Browning, 1812–89 – *Home Thoughts from Abroad*)

'She walks in beauty, like the night
Of cloudless climes and starry skies,
And all that's best of dark and bright
Meet in her aspect and her eyes'
(Lord Byron, 1788–1824 – *She Walks in Beauty*)

'I wander'd lonely as a cloud
That floats on high o'er vales and hills
When all at once I saw a crowd,
A host of golden daffodils'
(William Wordsworth, 1770–1850 – *The Daffodils*)

'Tyger! Tyger! Burning bright
In the forests of the night,
What immortal hand or eye
Could frame thy fearful symmetry?'
(William Blake, 1757–1827 – *The Tyger*)

'What passing-bells for these who die as cattle?
Only the monstrous anger of the guns.
Only the stuttering rifles' rapid rattle
Can patter out their hasty orisons.'
(Wilfred Owen, 1893–1918 – *Anthem for Doomed Youth*)

Check that you understand:

• Which sports are particularly popular in the UK

• Some of the major sporting events that take place each year

• Some of the major arts and culture events that happen in the UK

• How achievements in arts and culture are formally recognised

• Important figures in British literature

Leisure

People in the UK spend their leisure time in many different ways.

GARDENING

A lot of people have gardens at home and will spend their free time looking after them. Some people rent additional land called 'an allotment', where they grow fruit and vegetables. Gardening and flower shows range from major national exhibitions to small local events. Many towns have garden centres selling plants and gardening equipment. There are famous gardens to visit throughout the UK, including Kew Gardens, Sissinghurst and Hidcote in England, Crathes Castle and Inveraray Castle in Scotland, Bodnant Garden in Wales, and Mount Stewart in Northern Ireland.

The countries that make up the UK all have flowers which are particularly associated with them and which are sometimes worn on national saints' days:

England – the rose   *Scotland – the thistle*   *Wales – the daffodil*   *Northern Ireland – the shamrock*

SHOPPING

There are many different places to go shopping in the UK. Most towns and cities have a central shopping area, which is called the town centre. Undercover shopping centres are also common – these might be in town centres or on the outskirts of a town or city. Most shops in the UK are open seven days a week, although trading hours on Sundays and public holidays are generally reduced. Many towns also have markets on one or more days a week, where stallholders sell a variety of goods.

COOKING AND FOOD

Many people in the UK enjoy cooking. They often invite each other to their homes for dinner. A wide variety of food is eaten in the UK because of the country's rich cultural heritage and diverse population.

TRADITIONAL FOODS

There are a variety of foods that are traditionally associated with different parts of the UK:

England: Roast beef, which is served with potatoes, vegetables, Yorkshire puddings (batter that is baked in the oven) and other accompaniments. Fish and chips are also popular.

Wales: Welsh cakes – a traditional Welsh snack made from flour, dried fruits and spices, and served either hot or cold.

Scotland: Haggis – a sheep's stomach stuffed with offal, suet, onions and oatmeal.

Northern Ireland: Ulster fry – a fried meal with bacon, eggs, sausage, black pudding, white pudding, tomatoes, mushrooms, soda bread and potato bread.

FILMS

Eminent directors included Sir Alexander Korda and Sir Alfred Hitchcock, who later left for Hollywood and remained an important film director until his death in 1980.

British film industry

The UK has had a major influence on modern cinema.

Films were first shown publicly in the UK in 1896 and film screenings very quickly became popular. From the beginning, British film makers became famous for clever special effects and this continues to be an area of British expertise. From the early days of the cinema, British actors have worked in both the UK and USA. Sir Charles (Charlie) Chaplin became famous in silent movies for his tramp character and was one of many British actors to make a career in Hollywood.

British studios flourished in the 1930s. Eminent directors included Sir Alexander Korda and Sir Alfred Hitchcock, who later left for Hollywood and remained an important film director until his death in 1980. During the Second World War, British movies (for example, *In Which We Serve*) played an important part in boosting morale. Later, British directors including Sir David Lean and Ridley Scott found great success both in the UK and internationally.

The 1950s and 1960s were a high point for British comedies, including *Passport to Pimlico*, *The Ladykillers* and, later, the *Carry On* films.

Many of the films now produced in the UK are made by foreign companies, using British expertise. Some of the most commercially successful films of all time, including the two highest-grossing film franchises (Harry Potter and James Bond), have been produced in the UK. Ealing Studios has a claim to being the oldest continuously working film studio facility in the world. Britain continues to be particularly strong in special effects and animation. One example is the work of Nick Park, who has won four Oscars for his animated films, including three for films featuring Wallace and Gromit.

Actors such as Sir Laurence Olivier, David Niven, Sir Rex Harrison and Richard Burton starred in a wide variety of popular films. British actors continue to be popular and continue to win awards throughout the world. Recent British actors to have won Oscars include Colin Firth, Sir Anthony Hopkins, Dame Judi Dench, Kate Winslet and Tilda Swinton.

The annual British Academy Film Awards, hosted by the British Academy of Film and Television Arts (BAFTA), are the British equivalent of the Oscars.

> Actors such as Sir Laurence Olivier, David Niven, Sir Rex Harrison and Richard Burton starred in a wide variety of popular films.

SOME FAMOUS BRITISH FILMS

The 39 Steps (1935), directed by Alfred Hitchcock

Brief Encounter (1945), directed by David Lean

The Third Man (1949), directed by Carol Reed

The Belles of St Trinian's (1954), directed by Frank Launder

Lawrence of Arabia (1962), directed by David Lean

Women in Love (1969), directed by Ken Russell

Don't Look Now (1973), directed by Nicolas Roeg

Chariots of Fire (1981), directed by Hugh Hudson

The Killing Fields (1984), directed by Roland Joffé

Four Weddings and a Funeral (1994), directed by Mike Newell

Touching the Void (2003), directed by Kevin MacDonald.

You may be asked questions about these films and their directors, as well as the history of British cinema and famous actors.

BRITISH COMEDY

The traditions of comedy and satire, and the ability to laugh at ourselves, are an important part of the UK character.

Medieval kings and rich nobles had jesters who told jokes and made fun of people in the Court. Later, Shakespeare included comic characters in his plays. In the 18th century, political cartoons attacking prominent politicians – and, sometimes, the monarch or other members of the Royal Family – became increasingly popular. In the 19th century, satirical magazines began to be published. The most famous was *Punch*, which was published for the first time in the 1840s. Today, political cartoons continue to be published in newspapers, and magazines such as *Private Eye* continue the tradition of satire.

Comedians were a popular feature of British music hall, a form of variety theatre which was very common until television became the leading form of entertainment in the UK. Some of the people who had performed in the music halls in the 1940s and 1950s, such as Morecambe and Wise, became stars of television.

In the 19th century, satirical magazines began to be published. The most famous was Punch, which was published for the first time in the 1840s.

Television comedy developed its own style. Situation comedies, or sitcoms, which often look at family life and relationships in the workplace, remain popular. Satire has also continued to be important, with shows like *That Was The Week That Was* in the 1960s and *Spitting Image* in the 1980s and 1990s. In 1969, *Monty Python's Flying Circus* introduced a new type of progressive comedy. Stand-up comedy, where a solo comedian talks to a live audience, has become popular again in recent years.

TELEVISION AND RADIO

Many different television (TV) channels are available in the UK. Some are free to watch and others require a paid subscription. British television shows a wide variety of programmes. Popular programmes include regular soap operas such as *Coronation Street* and *EastEnders*. In Scotland, some Scotland-specific programmes are shown and there is also a channel with programmes in the Gaelic language. There is a Welsh-language channel in Wales. There are also programmes specific to Northern Ireland and some programmes broadcast in Irish Gaelic.

Everyone in the UK with a TV, computer or other medium which can be used for watching TV must have a television licence. One licence covers all of the equipment in one home, except when people rent different rooms in a shared house and each has a separate tenancy agreement – those people must each buy a separate licence. People over 75 can apply for a free TV licence and blind people can get a 50% discount. You will receive a fine of up to £1,000 if you watch TV but do not have a TV licence.

The money from TV licences is used to pay for the British Broadcasting Corporation (BBC). This is a British public service broadcaster providing television and radio programmes. The BBC is the largest broadcaster in the world. It is the only wholly state-funded media organisation that is independent of government. Other UK channels are primarily funded through advertisements and subscriptions.

There are also many different radio stations in the UK. Some broadcast nationally and others in certain cities or regions. There are radio stations that play certain types of music and some broadcast in regional languages such as Welsh or Gaelic. Like television, BBC radio stations are funded by TV licences and other radio stations are funded through advertisements.

SOCIAL NETWORKING

Social networking websites such as Facebook and Twitter are a popular way for people to stay in touch with friends, organise social events, and share photos, videos and opinions. Many people use social networking on their mobile phones when out and about.

PUBS AND NIGHT CLUBS

Public houses (pubs) are an important part of the UK social culture. Many people enjoy meeting friends in the pub. Most communities will have a 'local' pub that is a natural focal point for social activities. Pub quizzes are popular. Pool and darts are traditional pub games. To buy alcohol in a pub or night club you must be 18 or over, but people under that age may be allowed in some pubs with an adult. When they are 16, people can drink wine or beer with a meal in a hotel or restaurant (including eating areas in pubs) as long as they are with someone over 18.

Pubs are usually open during the day from 11.00 am (12 noon on Sundays). Night clubs with dancing and music usually open and close later than pubs. The licensee decides the hours that the pub or night club is open.

BETTING AND GAMBLING

In the UK, people often enjoy a gamble on sports or other events. There are also casinos in many places. You have to be 18 to go

> " The money from TV licences is used to pay for the British Broadcasting Corporation (BBC). This is a British public service broadcaster providing television and radio programmes. "

into betting shops or gambling clubs. There is a National Lottery for which draws are made every week. You can enter by buying a ticket or a scratch card. People under 16 are not allowed to participate in the National Lottery.

PETS

A lot of people in the UK have pets such as cats or dogs. They might have them for company or because they enjoy looking after them. It is against the law to treat a pet cruelly or to neglect it. All dogs in public places must wear a collar showing the name and address of the owner. The owner is responsible for keeping the dog under control and for cleaning up after the animal in a public place.

Vaccinations and medical treatment for animals are available from veterinary surgeons (vets). There are charities which may help people who cannot afford to pay a vet.

> The National Trust was founded in 1895 by three volunteers. There are now more than 61,000 volunteers helping to keep the organisation running.

Places of interest

The UK has a large network of public footpaths in the countryside. There are also many opportunities for mountain biking, mountaineering and hill walking. There are 15 national parks in England, Wales and Scotland. They are areas of protected countryside that everyone can visit, and where people live, work and look after the landscape.

There are many museums in the UK, which range from small community museums to large national and civic collections. Famous landmarks exist in towns, cities and the countryside throughout the UK. Most of them are open to the public to view (generally for a charge).

Many parts of the countryside and places of interest are kept open by the National Trust in England, Wales and Northern Ireland and the National Trust for Scotland. Both are charities that work to preserve important buildings, coastline and countryside in the UK. The National Trust was founded in 1895 by three volunteers. There are now more than 61,000 volunteers helping to keep the organisation running.

UK LANDMARKS

Big Ben

Big Ben is the nickname for the great bell of the clock at the Houses of Parliament in London. Many people call the clock Big Ben as well. The clock is over 150 years old and is a popular tourist attraction. The clock tower is named 'Elizabeth Tower' in honour of Queen Elizabeth II's Diamond Jubilee in 2012.

The Eden Project

The Eden Project is located in Cornwall, in the south west of England. Its biomes, which are like giant greenhouses, house plants from all over the world. The Eden Project is also a charity which runs environmental and social projects internationally.

Edinburgh Castle

The Castle is a dominant feature of the skyline in Edinburgh, Scotland. It has a long history, dating back to the early Middle Ages. It is looked after by Historic Scotland, a Scottish government agency.

The Giant's Causeway

Located on the north-east coast of Northern Ireland, the Giant's Causeway is a land formation of columns made from volcanic lava. It was formed about 50 million years ago. There are many legends about the Causeway and how it was formed.

Loch Lomond and the Trossachs National Park

This national park covers 720 square miles (1,865 square kilometres) in the west of Scotland. Loch Lomond is the largest expanse of fresh water in mainland Britain and probably the best-known part of the park.

© Sean Gallagher/National Geographic Society/Corbis

London Eye

The London Eye is situated on the southern bank of the River Thames and is a Ferris wheel that is 443 feet (135 metres) tall. It was originally built as part of the UK's celebration of the new millennium and continues to be an important part of New Year celebrations.

Snowdonia

Snowdonia is a national park in North Wales. It covers an area of 838 square miles (2,170 square kilometres). Its most well-known landmark is Snowdon, which is the highest mountain in Wales.

The Tower of London

The Tower of London was first built by William the Conqueror after he became king in 1066. Tours are given by the Yeoman Warders, also known as Beefeaters, who tell visitors about the building's history. People can also see the Crown Jewels there.

The Lake District

The Lake District is England's largest national park. It covers 885 square miles (2,292 square kilometres). It is famous for its lakes and mountains and is very popular with climbers, walkers and sailors. The biggest stretch of water is Windermere. In 2007, television viewers voted Wastwater as Britain's favourite view.

Check that you understand:

- Some of the ways in which people in the UK spend their leisure time
- The development of British cinema
- What the television licence is and how it funds the BBC
- Some of the places of interest to visit in the UK

CHAPTER 6
The UK government, the law and your role

→ IN THIS CHAPTER you will learn how the UK is governed. You need to understand the Queen's role in government and her powers. Make sure you understand how people are appointed to the two Houses of Parliament and the specific roles detailed, such as the Speaker and cabinet, and your rights to vote and stand for election. Everyone should understand the workings of the devolved administrations but pay particular attention if you are taking the test in Scotland, Wales or Northern Ireland.

The UK's international role is explained through the Commonwealth, EU and others so focus on the differences between these bodies and their member countries. The chapter then explains common laws, fundamental rights, policing and the courts of the UK. Pay particular attention to this so you know the differences between the various courts and offences they deal with. Finally the chapter deals with taxation, driving and community activity.

IN THIS CHAPTER THERE IS INFORMATION ABOUT:

- Britain as a constitutional monarchy
- How Parliament works
- Elections, the government and the opposition
- Devolved administrations of the UK
- The Commonwealth, EU, UN and NATO

- British law and justice
- The courts
- Fundamental principles and rights
- Tax
- Driving
- Community work and getting involved

The UK is a parliamentary democracy with the monarch as head of state. This section will tell you about the different institutions which make up this democratic system and explain how you can play a part in the democratic process.

The development of British democracy

Democracy is a system of government where the whole adult population gets a say. This might be by direct voting or by choosing representatives to make decisions on their behalf.

The voting franchise was also extended to women over 30, and then in 1928 to men and women over 21. In 1969, the voting age was reduced to 18 for men and women.

At the turn of the 19th century, Britain was not a democracy as we know it today. Although there were elections to select members of Parliament (MPs), only a small group of people could vote. They were men who were over 21 years of age and who owned a certain amount of property.

The franchise (that is, the number of people who had the right to vote) grew over the course of the 19th century and political parties began to involve ordinary men and women as members.

In the 1830s and 1840s, a group called the Chartists campaigned for reform. They wanted six changes:

- for every man to have the vote
- elections every year
- for all regions to be equal in the electoral system
- secret ballots
- for any man to be able to stand as an MP
- for MPs to be paid.

At the time, the campaign was generally seen as a failure. However, by 1918 most of these reforms had been adopted. The voting franchise was also extended to women over 30, and then in 1928 to men and women over 21. In 1969, the voting age was reduced to 18 for men and women.

The British constitution

A constitution is a set of principles by which a country is governed. It includes all of the institutions that are responsible for running the country and how their power is kept in check. The constitution also includes laws and conventions. The British constitution is not written down in any single document, and therefore it is described as 'unwritten'. This is mainly because the UK, unlike America or France, has never had a revolution which led permanently to a totally new system of government. Our most important institutions have developed over hundreds of years. Some people believe that there should be a single document, but others believe an unwritten constitution allows for more flexibility and better government.

CONSTITUTIONAL INSTITUTIONS

In the UK, there are several different parts of government. The main ones are:

- the monarchy
- Parliament (the House of Commons and the House of Lords)
- the Prime Minister
- the cabinet
- the judiciary (courts)
- the police
- the civil service
- local government.

In addition, there are devolved governments in Scotland, Wales and Northern Ireland that have the power to legislate on certain issues.

> The British constitution is not written down in any single document, and therefore it is described as 'unwritten'.

THE MONARCHY

Queen Elizabeth II is the head of state of the UK. She is also the monarch or head of state for many countries in the Commonwealth. The UK has a constitutional monarchy. This means that the king or queen does not rule the country but appoints the government, which the people have chosen in a democratic election. The monarch invites the leader of the party with the largest number of MPs, or the leader of a coalition between more than one party, to become the Prime Minister. The monarch has regular meetings with the Prime Minister and can advise, warn and encourage, but the decisions on government policies are made by the Prime Minister and cabinet (see the section on 'The government').

Queen Elizabeth II, head of state of the UK

© Getty Images

The Queen has reigned since her father's death in 1952, and in 2012 she celebrated her Diamond Jubilee (60 years as queen). She is married to Prince Philip, the Duke of Edinburgh. Her eldest son, Prince Charles (the Prince of Wales), is the heir to the throne.

The Queen has important ceremonial roles, such as the opening of the new parliamentary session each year. On this occasion the Queen makes a speech which summarises the government's policies for the year ahead. All Acts of Parliament are made in her name.

The Queen represents the UK to the rest of the world. She receives foreign ambassadors and high commissioners, entertains visiting heads of state, and makes state visits overseas in support of diplomatic and economic relationships with other countries.

The Queen has an important role in providing stability and continuity. While governments and Prime Ministers change regularly, the Queen continues as head of state. She provides a focus for national identity and pride, which was demonstrated through the celebrations of her Jubilee.

THE NATIONAL ANTHEM

The National Anthem of the UK is 'God Save the Queen'. It is played at important national occasions and at events attended by the Queen or the Royal Family. The first verse is:

> 'God save our gracious Queen!
> Long live our noble Queen!
> God save the Queen!
> Send her victorious,
> Happy and glorious,
> Long to reign over us,
> God save the Queen!'

New citizens swear or affirm loyalty to the Queen as part of the citizenship ceremony.

Oath of allegiance

'I (name) swear by Almighty God that on becoming a British citizen, I will be faithful and bear true allegiance to Her Majesty Queen Elizabeth the Second, her Heirs and Successors, according to law.'

Affirmation of allegiance

'I (name) do solemnly, sincerely and truly declare and affirm that on becoming a British citizen, I will be faithful and bear true allegiance to Her Majesty Queen Elizabeth the Second, her Heirs and Successors, according to law.'

> **"** The Queen has important ceremonial roles, such as the opening of the new parliamentary session each year. On this occasion the Queen makes a speech which summarises the government's policies for the year ahead. **"**

SYSTEM OF GOVERNMENT

The system of government in the UK is a parliamentary democracy. The UK is divided into parliamentary constituencies. Voters in each constituency elect their member of Parliament (MP) in a General Election. All of the elected MPs form the House of Commons. Most MPs belong to a political party, and the party with the majority of MPs forms the government. If one party does not get a majority, two parties can join together to form a coalition.

The Houses of Parliament, one of the centres of political life in the UK and a World Heritage Site

THE HOUSE OF COMMONS

The House of Commons is regarded as the more important of the two chambers in Parliament because its members are democratically elected. The Prime Minister and almost all the members of the cabinet are members of the House of Commons (MPs). Each MP represents a parliamentary constituency, which is a small area of the country. MPs have a number of different responsibilities. They:

- represent everyone in their constituency
- help to create new laws
- scrutinise and comment on what the government is doing
- debate important national issues.

THE HOUSE OF LORDS

Members of the House of Lords, known as peers, are not elected by the people and do not represent a constituency. The role and membership of the House of Lords has changed over the last 50 years.

Until 1958, all peers were:

• 'hereditary', which means they inherited their title, or

• senior judges, or

• bishops of the Church of England.

Since 1958, the Prime Minister has had the power to nominate peers just for their own lifetime. These are called life peers. They have usually had an important career in politics, business, law or another profession. Life peers are appointed by the monarch on the advice of the Prime Minister. They also include people nominated by the leaders of the other main political parties or by an independent Appointments Commission for non-party peers.

Since 1999, hereditary peers have lost the automatic right to attend the House of Lords. They now elect a few of their number to represent them in the House of Lords.

> Since 1999, hereditary peers have lost the automatic right to attend the House of Lords. They now elect a few of their number to represent them in the House of Lords.

The House of Lords is normally more independent of the government than the House of Commons. It can suggest amendments or propose new laws, which are then discussed by MPs. The House of Lords checks laws that have been passed by the House of Commons to ensure they are fit for purpose. It also holds the government to account to make sure that it is working in the best interests of the people. There are peers who are specialists in particular areas, and their knowledge is useful in making and checking laws. The House of Commons has powers to overrule the House of Lords, but these are not used often.

THE SPEAKER

Debates in the House of Commons are chaired by the Speaker. This person is the chief officer of the House of Commons. The Speaker is neutral and does not represent a political party, even though he or she is an MP, represents a constituency and deals with constituents' problems like any other MP. The Speaker is chosen by other MPs in a secret ballot.

The Speaker keeps order during political debates to make sure the rules are followed. This includes making sure the opposition (see the section on 'The government') has a guaranteed amount of time to debate issues which it chooses. The Speaker also represents Parliament on ceremonial occasions.

ELECTIONS

UK elections

MPs are elected at a General Election, which is held at least every five years.

If an MP dies or resigns, there will be a fresh election, called a by-election, in his or her constituency.

MPs are elected through a system called 'first past the post'. In each constituency, the candidate who gets the most votes is elected. The government is usually formed by the party that wins the majority of constituencies. If no party wins a majority, two parties may join together to form a coalition.

European parliamentary elections

Elections for the European Parliament are also held every five years. Elected members are called members of the European Parliament (MEPs). Elections to the European Parliament use a system of proportional representation, where seats are allocated to each party in proportion to the total number of votes it has won.

Elections to the European Parliament use a system of proportional representation, where seats are allocated to each party in proportion to the total number of votes it has won.

CONTACTING ELECTED MEMBERS

All elected members have a duty to serve and represent their constituents. You can get contact details for all your representatives and their parties from your local library and from www.parliament.uk. MPs, Assembly members, members of the Scottish Parliament (MSPs) and MEPs are also listed in *The Phone Book*, published by BT, and in *Yellow Pages*.

The House of Commons phone number is now 020 7219 4272

You can contact MPs by letter or telephone at their constituency office, or at their office in the House of Commons: The House of Commons, Westminster, London SW1A 0AA, telephone 020 7729 3000. In addition, many MPs, Assembly members, MSPs and MEPs hold regular local 'surgeries', where constituents can go in person to talk about issues that are of concern to them. These surgeries are often advertised in the local newspaper.

Check that you understand:

- How democracy has developed in the UK
- What a constitution is and how the UK's constitution is different from those of most other countries
- The role of the monarch
- The role of the House of Commons and House of Lords
- What the Speaker does
- How the UK elects MPs and MEPs

The government

THE PRIME MINISTER

The Prime Minister (PM) is the leader of the political party in power. He or she appoints the members of the cabinet (see below) and has control over many important public appointments. The official home of the Prime Minister is 10 Downing Street, in central London, near the Houses of Parliament. He or she also has a country house outside London called Chequers.

The Prime Minister can be changed if the MPs in the governing party decide to do so, or if he or she wishes to resign. The Prime Minister usually resigns if his or her party loses a General Election.

THE CABINET

The Prime Minister appoints about 20 senior MPs to become ministers in charge of departments. These include:

- Chancellor of the Exchequer – responsible for the economy
- Home Secretary – responsible for crime, policing and immigration
- Foreign Secretary – responsible for managing relationships with foreign countries
- other ministers (called 'Secretaries of State') responsible for subjects such as education, health and defence.

These ministers form the cabinet, a committee which usually meets weekly and makes important decisions about government policy. Many of these decisions have to be debated or approved by Parliament.

Each department also has a number of other ministers, called Ministers of State and Parliamentary Under-Secretaries of State, who take charge of particular areas of the department's work.

THE OPPOSITION

The second-largest party in the House of Commons is called the opposition. The leader of the opposition usually becomes Prime Minister if his or her party wins the next General Election.

The leader of the opposition leads his or her party in pointing out what they see as the government's failures and weaknesses. One important opportunity to do this is at Prime Minister's Questions, which takes place every week while Parliament is sitting. The leader of the opposition also appoints senior opposition MPs to be 'shadow ministers'. They form the shadow cabinet and their role is to challenge the government and put forward alternative policies.

> There are a few MPs who do not represent any of the main political parties. They are called 'independents' and usually represent an issue important to their constituency.

THE PARTY SYSTEM

Anyone aged 18 or over can stand for election as an MP but they are unlikely to win unless they have been nominated to represent one of the major political parties. These are the Conservative Party, the Labour Party, the Liberal Democrats, or one of the parties representing Scottish, Welsh or Northern Irish interests.

There are a few MPs who do not represent any of the main political parties. They are called 'independents' and usually represent an issue important to their constituency.

The main political parties actively look for members of the public to join their debates, contribute to their costs, and help at elections for Parliament or for local government. They have branches in most constituencies and hold policy-making conferences every year.

Pressure and lobby groups are organisations which try to influence government policy. They play an important role in politics. Some are representative organisations such as the CBI (Confederation of British Industry), which represents the views of British business. Others campaign on particular topics, such as the environment (for example, Greenpeace) or human rights (for example, Liberty).

THE CIVIL SERVICE

Civil servants support the government in developing and implementing its policies. They also deliver public services. Civil servants are accountable to ministers. They are chosen on merit and are politically neutral – they are not political appointees. People can apply to join the civil service through an application process, like other jobs in the UK. Civil servants are expected to carry out their role with dedication and a commitment to the civil service and its core values. These are: integrity, honesty, objectivity and impartiality (including being politically neutral).

LOCAL GOVERNMENT

Towns, cities and rural areas in the UK are governed by democratically elected councils, often called 'local authorities'. Some areas have both district and county councils, which have different functions. Most large towns and cities have a single local authority.

Local authorities provide a range of services in their areas. They are funded by money from central government and by local taxes.

Many local authorities appoint a mayor, who is the ceremonial leader of the council. In some towns, a mayor is elected to be the effective leader of the administration. London has 33 local authorities, with the Greater London Authority and the Mayor of London coordinating policies across the capital. For most local authorities, local elections for councillors are held in May every year. Many candidates stand for council election as members of a political party.

Civil servants are accountable to ministers. They are chosen on merit and are politically neutral – they are not political appointees.

DEVOLVED ADMINISTRATIONS

Since 1997, some powers have been devolved from the central government to give people in Wales, Scotland and Northern Ireland more control over matters that directly affect them. There has been a Welsh Assembly and a Scottish Parliament since 1999. There is also a Northern Ireland Assembly, although this has been suspended on a few occasions.

Policy and laws governing defence, foreign affairs, immigration, taxation and social security all remain under central UK government control. However, many other public services, such as education, are controlled by the devolved administrations.

The devolved administrations each have their own civil service.

Devolved administrations of the UK

The Welsh Assembly

Formed in 1999 in Cardiff, capital of Wales
Members: 60 AMs
Elections: Every four years
Powers: Since 2011 can make law without UK Parliament in 20 areas including:
• education and training
• health and social services
• economic development
• housing

The Scottish Parliament

Formed in 1999 in Edinburgh
Members: 129 MSPs
Elections: Use a form of proportional representation
Powers: In all areas not specifically reserved by UK Parliament (see above), including:
• civil and criminal law
• health
• education
• planning
• additional tax-raising powers

The Northern Ireland Parliament

First established in 1922
Abolished in 1972, after The Troubles started in 1969

The Northern Ireland Assembly

Established after the Belfast Agreement in 1998
Members: 108 MLAs
Elections: Use a form of proportional representation. Ministerial offices shared between main parties
Powers: In areas including:
• education
• agriculture
• the environment
• health
• social services
Has been suspended several times, but running uninterrupted since 2007

The Welsh government

The Welsh government and National Assembly for Wales are based in Cardiff, the capital city of Wales. The National Assembly has 60 Assembly members (AMs) and elections are held every four years using a form of proportional representation. Members can speak in either Welsh or English and all of the Assembly's publications are in both languages.

The Assembly has the power to make laws for Wales in 20 areas, including:

- education and training
- health and social services
- economic development
- housing.

Since 2011, the National Assembly for Wales has been able to pass laws on these topics without the agreement of the UK Parliament.

The Welsh Assembly building, opened in March 2006

The Scottish Parliament building, opened in October 2004

The Scottish Parliament

The Scottish Parliament was formed in 1999. It sits in Edinburgh, the capital city of Scotland.

There are 129 members of the Scottish Parliament (MSPs), elected by a form of proportional representation. The Scottish Parliament can pass laws for Scotland on all matters which are not specifically reserved to the UK Parliament. The matters on which the Scottish Parliament can legislate include:

> You should know about all of the devolved administrations, wherever you live in the UK. Make sure you know how they were formed and the powers they have.

- civil and criminal law
- health
- education
- planning
- additional tax-raising powers.

The Northern Ireland Assembly

A Northern Ireland Parliament was established in 1922, when Ireland was divided, but it was abolished in 1972, shortly after the Troubles broke out in 1969 (see pages 47–8).

The Northern Ireland Assembly was established soon after the Belfast Agreement (or Good Friday Agreement) in 1998. There is a power-sharing agreement which distributes ministerial offices amongst the main parties. The Assembly has 108 elected members, known as MLAs (members of the Legislative Assembly). They are elected with a form of proportional representation.

The Northern Ireland Assembly, known as Stormont

The Northern Ireland Assembly can make decisions on issues such as:

• education
• agriculture
• the environment
• health
• social services.

The UK government has the power to suspend all devolved assemblies. It has used this power several times in Northern Ireland when local political leaders found it difficult to work together. However, the Assembly has been running successfully since 2007.

THE MEDIA AND GOVERNMENT

Proceedings in Parliament are broadcast on television and published in official reports called *Hansard*. Written reports can be found in large libraries and at www.parliament.uk. Most people get information about political issues and events from newspapers (often called 'the press'), television, radio and the internet.

The UK has a free press. This means that what is written in newspapers is free from government control. Some newspaper owners and editors hold strong political opinions and run campaigns to try to influence government policy and public opinion.

By law, radio and television coverage of the political parties must be balanced and so equal time has to be given to rival viewpoints.

Proceedings in Parliament are broadcast on television and published in official reports called *Hansard*.

Check that you understand:

• The role of the Prime Minister, cabinet, opposition and shadow cabinet

• The role of political parties in the UK system of government

• Who the main political parties are

• What pressure and lobby groups do

• The role of the civil service

• The role of local government

• The powers of the devolved governments in Wales, Scotland and Northern Ireland

• How proceedings in Parliament are recorded

• The role of the media in keeping people informed about political issues

Who can vote?

The UK has had a fully democratic voting system since 1928 (see page 106). The present voting age of 18 was set in 1969 and (with a few exceptions) all UK-born and naturalised adult citizens have the right to vote.

Adult citizens of the UK, and citizens of the Commonwealth and the Irish Republic who are resident in the UK, can vote in all public elections. Adult citizens of other EU states who are resident in the UK can vote in all elections except General Elections.

THE ELECTORAL REGISTER

To be able to vote in a parliamentary, local or European election, you must have your name on the electoral register.

If you are eligible to vote, you can register by contacting your local council electoral registration office. This is usually based at your local council (in Scotland it may be based elsewhere). If you don't know which local authority you come under, you can find out by visiting www.aboutmyvote.co.uk and entering your postcode. You can also download voter registration forms in English, Welsh and some other languages.

The electoral register is updated every year in September or October. An electoral registration form is sent to every household and this has to be completed and returned with the names of everyone who is resident in the household and eligible to vote.

In Northern Ireland a different system operates. This is called 'individual registration' and all those entitled to vote must complete their own registration form. Once registered, people stay on the register provided their personal details do not change. For more information see the Electoral Office for Northern Ireland website at www.eoni.org.uk.

By law, each local authority has to make its electoral register available for anyone to look at, although this has to be supervised. The register is kept at each local electoral registration office (or council office in England and Wales). It is also possible to see the register at some public buildings such as libraries.

WHERE TO VOTE

People vote in elections at places called polling stations, or polling places in Scotland. Before the election you will be sent a poll card. This tells you where your polling station or polling place is and when the election will take place. On election day, the polling station or place will be open from 7.00 am until 10.00 pm.

When you arrive at the polling station, the staff will ask for your name and address. In Northern Ireland you will also have to show photographic identification. You will then get your ballot paper, which you take to a polling booth to fill in privately. You should make up your own mind who to vote for. No one has the right to make you vote for a particular candidate. You should follow the instructions on the ballot paper. Once you have completed it, put it in the ballot box.

If it is difficult for you to get to a polling station or polling place, you can register for a postal ballot. Your ballot paper will be sent to your home before the election. You then fill it in and post it back. You can choose to do this when you register to vote.

> **"** By law, each local authority has to make its electoral register available for anyone to look at, although this has to be supervised. **"**

STANDING FOR OFFICE

Most citizens of the UK, the Irish Republic or the Commonwealth aged 18 or over can stand for public office. There are some exceptions, including:

- members of the armed forces
- civil servants
- people found guilty of certain criminal offences.

Members of the House of Lords may not stand for election to the House of Commons but are eligible for all other public offices.

VISITING PARLIAMENT AND THE DEVOLVED ADMINISTRATIONS

The UK Parliament

The public can listen to debates in the Palace of Westminster from public galleries in both the House of Commons and the House of Lords.

You can write to your local MP in advance to ask for tickets or you can queue on the day at the public entrance. Entrance is free. Sometimes there are long queues for the House of Commons and people have to wait for at least one to two hours. It is usually easier to get in to the House of Lords.

You can find further information on the UK Parliament website at www.parliament.uk.

Northern Ireland Assembly

In Northern Ireland elected members, known as MLAs, meet in the Northern Ireland Assembly at Stormont, in Belfast.

There are two ways to arrange a visit to Stormont. You can either contact the Education Service (details are on the Northern Ireland Assembly website at www.niassembly.gov.uk) or contact an MLA.

Scottish Parliament

In Scotland the elected members, called MSPs, meet in the Scottish Parliament building at Holyrood in Edinburgh (for more information, see www.scottish.parliament.uk).

You can get information, book tickets or arrange tours through visitor services. You can write to them at the Scottish Parliament, Edinburgh, EH99 1SP, telephone 0131 348 5200 or email sp.bookings@scottish.parliament.uk.

The Welsh Assembly site is now www.gov.wales

National Assembly for Wales

In Wales the elected members, known as AMs, meet in the Welsh Assembly in the Senedd in Cardiff Bay (for more information, see www.wales.gov.uk).

The Senedd is an open building. You can book guided tours or seats in the public galleries for the Welsh Assembly. To make a booking, contact the Assembly Booking Service on 0845 010 5500 or email assembly.bookings@wales.gsi.gov.uk.

Check that you understand:

- Who is eligible to vote

- How you register to vote

- How to vote

- Who can stand for public office

- How you can visit Parliament, the Northern Ireland Assembly, the Scottish Parliament and the Welsh Assembly

The UK and international institutions

THE COMMONWEALTH

The Commonwealth is an association of countries that support each other and work together towards shared goals in democracy and development. Most member states were once part of the British Empire, although a few countries which were not have also joined.

The Queen is the ceremonial head of the Commonwealth, which currently has 53 member states (see table below). Membership is voluntary. The Commonwealth has no power over its members, although it can suspend membership. The Commonwealth is based on the core values of democracy, good government and the rule of law.

Commonwealth members

Antigua and Barbuda	Australia	The Bahamas
Bangladesh	Barbados	Belize
Botswana	Brunei Darussalam	Cameroon
Canada	Cyprus	Dominica

Fiji (currently suspended)	Ghana	Grenada
Guyana	India	Jamaica
Kenya	Kiribati	Lesotho
Malawi	Malaysia	Maldives
Malta	Mauritius	Mozambique
Namibia	Nauru	New Zealand
Nigeria	Pakistan	Papua New Guinea
Rwanda	Samoa	Seychelles
Sierra Leone	Singapore	Solomon Islands
South Africa	Sri Lanka	St Kitts and Nevis
St Lucia	St Vincent and the Grenadines	Swaziland
Tanzania	Tonga	Trinidad and Tobago
Tuvalu	Uganda	UK
Vanuatu	Zambia	

Note that The Gambia left the commonwealth in October 2013.

THE EUROPEAN UNION

The European Union (EU), originally called the European Economic Community (EEC), was set up by six western European countries (Belgium, France, Germany, Italy, Luxembourg and the Netherlands) who signed the Treaty of Rome on 25 March 1957. The UK originally decided not to join this group but it became a member in 1973. There are now 28 EU member states (see table below). Croatia became a member state in 2013.

EU member states

Austria	Belgium	Bulgaria	Croatia
Cyprus	Czech Republic	Denmark	Estonia
Finland	France	Germany	Greece
Hungary	Ireland	Italy	Latvia
Lithuania	Luxembourg	Malta	Netherlands

Poland	Portugal	Romania	Slovakia
Slovenia	Spain	Sweden	UK

EU law is legally binding in the UK and all the other EU member states. European laws are called directives, regulations or framework decisions.

THE COUNCIL OF EUROPE

The Council of Europe is separate from the EU. It has 47 member countries, including the UK, and is responsible for the protection and promotion of human rights in those countries. It has no power to make laws but draws up conventions and charters, the most well-known of which is the European Convention on Human Rights and Fundamental Freedoms, usually called the European Convention on Human Rights.

THE UNITED NATIONS

The UK is part of the United Nations (UN), an international organisation with more than 190 countries as members.

The UN was set up after the Second World War and aims to prevent war and promote international peace and security. There are 15 members on the UN Security Council, which recommends action when there are international crises and threats to peace. The UK is one of five permanent members of the Security Council.

The Council of Europe is separate from the EU. It has 47 member countries.

THE NORTH ATLANTIC TREATY ORGANIZATION (NATO)

The UK is also a member of NATO. NATO is a group of European and North American countries that have agreed to help each other if they come under attack. It also aims to maintain peace between all of its members.

Check that you understand:

• What the Commonwealth is and its role

• Other international organisations of which the UK is a member

Respecting the law

One of the most important responsibilities of all residents in the UK is to know and obey the law. This section will tell you about the legal system in the UK and some of the laws that may affect you. Britain is proud of being a welcoming country, but all residents, regardless of their background, are expected to comply with the law and to understand that some things which may be allowed in other legal systems are not acceptable in the UK. Those who do not respect the law should not expect to be allowed to become permanent residents in the UK.

The law is relevant to all areas of life in the UK. You should make sure that you are aware of the laws which affect your everyday life, including both your personal and business affairs.

 Every person in the UK receives equal treatment under the law. This means that the law applies in the same way to everyone, no matter who they are or where they are from.

THE LAW IN THE UK

Every person in the UK receives equal treatment under the law. This means that the law applies in the same way to everyone, no matter who they are or where they are from.

Laws can be divided into criminal law and civil law:

- Criminal law relates to crimes, which are usually investigated by the police or another authority such as a council, and which are punished by the courts.
- Civil law is used to settle disputes between individuals or groups.

Examples of criminal laws are:

- Carrying a weapon: it is a criminal offence to carry a weapon of any kind, even if it is for self-defence. This includes a gun, a knife or anything that is made or adapted to cause injury.
- Drugs: selling or buying drugs such as heroin, cocaine, ecstasy and cannabis is illegal in the UK.
- Racial crime: it is a criminal offence to cause harassment, alarm or distress to someone because of their religion or ethnic origin.
- Selling tobacco: it is illegal to sell tobacco products (for example, cigarettes, cigars, roll-up tobacco) to anyone under the age of 18.
- Smoking in public places: it is against the law to smoke tobacco products in nearly every enclosed public place in the UK. There are signs displayed to tell you where you cannot smoke.

- Buying alcohol: it is a criminal offence to sell alcohol to anyone who is under 18 or to buy alcohol for people who are under the age of 18. (There is one exception: people aged 16 or over can drink alcohol with a meal in a hotel or restaurant – see page 93.)
- Drinking in public: some places have alcohol-free zones where you cannot drink in public. The police can also confiscate alcohol or move young people on from public places. You can be fined or arrested.

This list does not include all crimes. There are many that apply in most countries, such as murder, theft and assault. You can find out more about types of crime in the UK at www.gov.uk.

Examples of civil laws are:

- Housing law: this includes disputes between landlords and tenants over issues such as repairs and eviction.
- Consumer rights: an example of this is a dispute about faulty goods or services.
- Employment law: these cases include disputes over wages and cases of unfair dismissal or discrimination in the workplace.
- Debt: people might be taken to court if they owe money to someone.

THE POLICE AND THEIR DUTIES

The job of the police in the UK is to:

- protect life and property
- prevent disturbances (also known as keeping the peace)
- prevent and detect crime.

The police are organised into a number of separate police forces headed by Chief Constables. They are independent of the government.

In November 2012, the public elected Police and Crime Commissioners (PCCs) in England and Wales. These are directly elected individuals who are responsible for the delivery of an efficient and effective police force that reflects the needs of their local communities. PCCs set local police priorities and the local policing budget. They also appoint the Chief Constable.

66
PCCs set local police priorities and the local policing budget. They also appoint the Chief Constable.
99

The police in the UK protect life and property, prevent disturbances, and prevent and detect crime

© Peter Dazeley/Getty Images

The police force is a public service that helps and protects everyone, no matter what their background or where they live. Police officers must themselves obey the law. They must not misuse their authority, make a false statement, be rude or abusive, or commit racial discrimination. If police officers are corrupt or misuse their authority they are severely punished.

Police officers are supported by police community support officers (PCSOs). PCSOs have different roles according to the area but usually patrol the streets, work with the public, and support police officers at crime scenes and major events.

All people in the UK are expected to help the police prevent and detect crimes whenever they can. If you are arrested and taken to a police station, a police officer will tell you the reason for your arrest and you will be able to seek legal advice.

If something goes wrong, the police complaints system tries to put it right. Anyone can make a complaint about the police by going to a police station or writing to the Chief Constable of the police force involved. Complaints can also be made to an independent body: the Independent Police Complaints Commission in England and Wales, the Police Complaints Commissioner for Scotland or the Police Ombudsman for Northern Ireland.

TERRORISM AND EXTREMISM

The UK faces a range of terrorist threats. The most serious of these is from Al Qa'ida, its affiliates and like-minded organisations. The UK also faces threats from other kinds of terrorism, such as Northern Ireland-related terrorism.

All terrorist groups try to radicalise and recruit people to their cause. How, where and to what extent they try to do so will vary. Evidence shows that these groups attract very low levels of public support, but people who want to make their home in the UK should be aware of this threat. It is important that all citizens feel safe. This includes feeling safe from all kinds of extremism (vocal or active opposition to fundamental British values), including religious extremism and far-right extremism.

If you think someone is trying to persuade you to join an extremist or terrorist cause, you should notify your local police force.

Check that you understand:

- The difference between civil and criminal law and some examples of each
- The duties of the police
- The possible terrorist threats facing the UK

The role of the courts

THE JUDICIARY

Judges (who are together called 'the judiciary') are responsible for interpreting the law and ensuring that trials are conducted fairly. The government cannot interfere with this.

Sometimes the actions of the government are claimed to be illegal. If the judges agree, then the government must either change its policies or ask Parliament to change the law. If judges find that a public body is not respecting someone's legal rights, they can order that body to change its practices and/or pay compensation.

Judges also make decisions in disputes between members of the public or organisations. These might be about contracts, property or employment rights or after an accident.

CRIMINAL COURTS

There are some differences between the court systems in England and Wales, Scotland and Northern Ireland.

Magistrates' and Justice of the Peace Courts

In England, Wales and Northern Ireland, most minor criminal cases are dealt with in a Magistrates' Court. In Scotland, minor criminal offences go to a Justice of the Peace Court.

Magistrates and Justices of the Peace (JPs) are members of the local community. In England, Wales and Scotland they usually work unpaid and do not need legal qualifications. They receive training to do the job and are supported by a legal adviser. Magistrates decide the verdict in each case that comes before them and, if the person is found guilty, the sentence that they are given. In Northern Ireland, cases are heard by a District Judge or Deputy District Judge, who is legally qualified and paid.

> In England, Wales and Northern Ireland, serious offences are tried in front of a judge and a jury in a Crown Court.

Crown Courts and Sheriff Courts

In England, Wales and Northern Ireland, serious offences are tried in front of a judge and a jury in a Crown Court. In Scotland, serious cases are heard in a Sheriff Court with either a sheriff or a sheriff with a jury. The most serious cases in Scotland, such as murder, are heard at a High Court with a judge and jury. A jury is made up of members of the public chosen at random from the local electoral register (see pages 120–1). In England, Wales and Northern Ireland a jury has 12 members, and in Scotland a jury has 15 members. Everyone who is summoned to do jury service must do it unless they are not eligible (for example, because they have a criminal conviction) or they provide a good reason to be excused, such as ill health.

The jury has to listen to the evidence presented at the trial and then decide a verdict of 'guilty' or 'not guilty' based on what they have heard. In Scotland, a third verdict of 'not proven' is also possible. If the jury finds a defendant guilty, the judge decides on the penalty.

The Old Bailey is probably the most famous criminal court in the world

Youth Courts

In England, Wales and Northern Ireland, if an accused person is aged 10 to 17, the case is normally heard in a Youth Court in front of up to three specially trained magistrates or a District Judge. The most serious cases will go to the Crown Court. The parents or carers of the young person are expected to attend the hearing. Members of the public are not allowed in Youth Courts, and the name or photographs of the accused young person cannot be published in newspapers or used by the media.

In Scotland a system called the Children's Hearings System is used to deal with children and young people who have committed an offence.

Northern Ireland has a system of youth conferencing to consider how a child should be dealt with when they have committed an offence.

?

Make sure you understand the differences between criminal and civil law, and the crimes they deal with. This includes the types of case each court handles and the differences across the UK.

Criminal Courts

(Scotland only) Most serious offences, such as murder

Scotland: High Court
Cases are heard by judge and jury

Serious offences

England, Wales and Northern Ireland: Crown Court
Trials are before a judge and jury

Scotland: Sheriff Court
Trials are before a sheriff, or a sheriff and jury

Most minor criminal cases

England and Wales: Magistrates' Court
Magistrates are unpaid and do not need legal qualifications

Scotland: Justice of the Peace Court
Justices (JPs) are unpaid and do not need legal qualifications

Northern Ireland: Magistrates' Court
District Judges, or Deputy District Judges are legally qualified and paid

Youth Courts

England, Wales and Northern Ireland: Youth Court
• Where accused is aged 10–17
• Cases heard by up to three specially trained magistrates or a District Judge
• Most serious cases go to Crown Court
• Parents/Carers are expected to attend
• Closed courts – public cannot attend and names/photos of accused cannot be used by the media

Scotland: Children's Hearings System is used

Northern Ireland only: Youth conferencing system used to consider punishment/treatment of children

Juries of the UK

England, Wales and Northern Ireland – 12 members
Verdicts 'guilty' or 'not guilty'

Scotland – 15 members
Verdicts 'guilty', 'not guilty' or 'not proven'

CIVIL COURTS

County Courts

County Courts deal with a wide range of civil disputes. These include people trying to get back money that is owed to them, cases involving personal injury, family matters, breaches of contract, and divorce. In Scotland, most of these matters are dealt with in the Sheriff Court. More serious civil cases – for example, when a large amount of compensation is being claimed – are dealt with in the High Court in England, Wales and Northern Ireland. In Scotland, they are dealt with in the Court of Session in Edinburgh.

The small claims procedure

The small claims procedure is an informal way of helping people to settle minor disputes without spending a lot of time and money using a lawyer. This procedure is used for claims of less than £5,000 in England and Wales and £3,000 in Scotland and Northern Ireland. The hearing is held in front of a judge in an ordinary room, and people from both sides of the dispute sit around a table. Small claims can also be issued online through Money Claims Online (www.moneyclaim.gov.uk).

You can get details about the small claims procedure from your local County Court or Sheriff Court. Details of your local court can be found as follows:

• England and Wales: at www.gov.uk

• Scotland: at www.scotcourts.gov.uk

• Northern Ireland: at www.courtsni.gov.uk.

"
The small claims procedure is an informal way of helping people to settle minor disputes without spending a lot of time and money using a lawyer.
"

Civil Courts

Serious civil cases, e.g. large compensation claims

| England, Wales and Northern Ireland: High Court | Scotland: Court of Session, in Edinburgh |

Civil disputes, e.g. personal injury claims, family matters, breaches of contract and divorce

| England, Wales and Northern Ireland: County Courts | Scotland: Sheriff Court |

Small civil claims

| England and Wales: Small claims procedure for anything under £5,000 | Scotland and Ireland: Small claims procedure for anything under £3,000 |

Hearings are with judge and both parties around a table

All UK: Money Claims Online
Online alternative to the small claims procedure

LEGAL ADVICE

Solicitors

Solicitors are trained lawyers who give advice on legal matters, take action for their clients and represent their clients in court.

There are solicitors' offices throughout the UK. It is important to find out which aspects of law a solicitor specialises in and to check that they have the right experience to help you with your case. Many advertise in local newspapers and in *Yellow Pages*. The Citizens Advice Bureau (www.citizensadvice.org.uk) can give you names of local solicitors and which areas of law they specialise in. You can also get this information from the Law Society (www.lawsociety.org.uk) in England and Wales, the Law Society of Scotland (www.lawscot.org.uk) or the Law Society of Northern Ireland (www.lawsoc-ni.org). Solicitors' charges are usually based on how much time they spend on a case. It is very important to find out at the start how much a case is likely to cost.

Check that you understand:

- The role of the judiciary
- About the different criminal courts in the UK
- About the different civil courts in the UK
- How you can settle a small claim

Fundamental principles

Britain has a long history of respecting an individual's rights and ensuring essential freedoms. These rights have their roots in the Magna Carta, the Habeas Corpus Act and the Bill of Rights of 1689 (see pages 18–9, 30 and 33), and they have developed over a period of time. British diplomats and lawyers had an important role in drafting the European Convention on Human Rights and Fundamental Freedoms. The UK was one of the first countries to sign the Convention in 1950.

Some of the principles included in the European Convention on Human Rights are:

- right to life
- prohibition of torture
- prohibition of slavery and forced labour
- right to liberty and security
- right to a fair trial
- freedom of thought, conscience and religion
- freedom of expression (speech).

British diplomats and lawyers had an important role in drafting the European Convention on Human Rights and Fundamental Freedoms.

The Human Rights Act 1998 incorporated the European Convention on Human Rights into UK law. The government, public bodies and the courts must follow the principles of the Convention.

EQUAL OPPORTUNITIES

UK laws ensure that people are not treated unfairly in any area of life or work because of their age, disability, sex, pregnancy and maternity, race, religion or belief, sexuality or marital status. If you face problems with discrimination, you can get more information from the Citizens Advice Bureau or from one of the following organisations:

• England and Wales: Equality and Human Rights Commission (www.equalityhumanrights.com)

> Any man who forces a woman to have sex, including a woman's husband, can be charged with rape.

• Scotland: Equality and Human Rights Commission in Scotland (www.equalityhumanrights.com/scotland/the-commission-in-scotland) and Scottish Human Rights Commission (www.scottishhumanrights.com)

• Northern Ireland: Equality Commission for Northern Ireland (www.equalityni.org)

• Northern Ireland Human Rights Commission (www.nihrc.org).

DOMESTIC VIOLENCE

In the UK, brutality and violence in the home is a serious crime. Anyone who is violent towards their partner – whether they are a man or woman, married or living together – can be prosecuted. Any man who forces a woman to have sex, including a woman's husband, can be charged with rape.

It is important for anyone facing domestic violence to get help as soon as possible. A solicitor or the Citizens Advice Bureau can explain the available options. In some areas there are safe places to go and stay in, called refuges or shelters. There are emergency telephone numbers in the helpline section at the front of *Yellow Pages*, including, for women, the number of the nearest women's centre. You can also phone the 24-hour National Domestic Violence Freephone Helpline on 0808 2000 247 at any time, or the police can help you find a safe place to stay.

FEMALE GENITAL MUTILATION

Female genital mutilation (FGM), also known as cutting or female circumcision, is illegal in the UK. Practising FGM or taking a girl or woman abroad for FGM is a criminal offence.

FORCED MARRIAGE

A marriage should be entered into with the full and free consent of both people involved. Arranged marriages, where both parties agree to the marriage, are acceptable in the UK.

Forced marriage is where one or both parties do not or cannot give their consent to enter into the partnership. Forcing another person to marry is a criminal offence.

Forced Marriage Protection Orders were introduced in 2008 for England, Wales and Northern Ireland under the Forced Marriage (Civil Protection) Act 2007. Court orders can be obtained to protect a person from being forced into a marriage, or to protect a person in a forced marriage. Similar Protection Orders were introduced in Scotland in November 2011.

A potential victim, or someone acting for them, can apply for an order. Anyone found to have breached an order can be jailed for up to two years for contempt of court.

> **"** A marriage should be entered into with the full and free consent of both people involved. Arranged marriages, where both parties agree to the marriage, are acceptable in the UK. **"**

Taxation

INCOME TAX

People in the UK have to pay tax on their income, which includes:

- wages from paid employment
- profits from self-employment
- taxable benefits
- pensions
- income from property, savings and dividends.

Money raised from income tax pays for government services such as roads, education, police and the armed forces.

For most people, the right amount of income tax is automatically taken from their income from employment by their employer and

The HMRC sites are now found at www.gov.uk/ hmrc, /incometax and /national insurance. The self-assessment helpline number is now 0300 200 3310.

paid directly to HM Revenue & Customs (HMRC), the government department that collects taxes. This system is called 'Pay As You Earn' (PAYE). If you are self-employed, you need to pay your own tax through a system called 'self-assessment', which includes completing a tax return. Other people may also need to complete a tax return. If HMRC sends you a tax return, it is important to complete and return the form as soon as you have all the necessary information.

You can find out more about income tax at www.hmrc.gov. uk/incometax. You can get help and advice about taxes and completing tax forms from the HMRC self-assessment helpline, on 0845 300 0627, and the HMRC website at www.hmrc.gov.uk.

NATIONAL INSURANCE

The money raised from National Insurance Contributions is used to pay for state benefits and services such as the state retirement pension and the National Health Service (NHS).

Almost everybody in the UK who is in paid work, including self-employed people, must pay National Insurance Contributions. The money raised from National Insurance Contributions is used to pay for state benefits and services such as the state retirement pension and the National Health Service (NHS).

Employees have their National Insurance Contributions deducted from their pay by their employer. People who are self-employed need to pay National Insurance Contributions themselves.

Anyone who does not pay enough National Insurance Contributions will not be able to receive certain contributory benefits such as Jobseeker's Allowance or a full state retirement pension. Some workers, such as part-time workers, may not qualify for statutory payments such as maternity pay if they do not earn enough.

Further guidance about National Insurance Contributions is available on HMRC's website at www.hmrc.gov.uk/ni.

Getting a National Insurance number

A National Insurance number is a unique personal account number. It makes sure that the National Insurance Contributions and tax you pay are properly recorded against your name. All young people in the UK are sent a National Insurance number just before their 16th birthday.

A non-UK national living in the UK and looking for work, starting work or setting up as self-employed will need a National Insurance number. However, you can start work without one. If you have permission to work in the UK, you will need to telephone the

Department for Work and Pensions (DWP) to arrange to get a National Insurance number. You may be required to attend an interview. The DWP will advise you of the appropriate application process and tell you which documents you will need to bring to an interview if one is necessary. You will usually need documents that prove your identity and that you have permission to work in the UK. A National Insurance number does not on its own prove to an employer that you have the right to work in the UK.

You can find out more information about how to apply for a National Insurance number at www.gov.uk.

Driving

In the UK, you must be at least 17 years old to drive a car or motor cycle and you must have a driving licence to drive on public roads. To get a UK driving licence you must pass a driving test, which tests both your knowledge and your practical skills. You need to be at least 16 years old to ride a moped, and there are other age requirements and special tests for driving large vehicles.

Drivers can use their driving licence until they are 70 years old. After that, the licence is valid for three years at a time.

In Northern Ireland, a newly qualified driver must display an 'R' plate (for restricted driver) for one year after passing the test.

If your driving licence is from a country in the European Union (EU), Iceland, Liechtenstein or Norway, you can drive in the UK for as long as your licence is valid. If you have a licence from any other country, you may use it in the UK for up to 12 months. To continue driving after that, you must get a UK full driving licence.

If you are resident in the UK, your car or motor cycle must be registered at the Driver and Vehicle Licensing Agency (DVLA). You must pay an annual road tax and display the tax disc, which shows that the tax has been paid, on the windscreen. You must also have valid motor insurance. It is a serious criminal offence to drive without insurance. If your vehicle is over three years old, you must take it for a Ministry of Transport (MOT) test every year. It is an offence not to have an MOT certificate if your vehicle is more than three years old. You can find out more about vehicle tax and MOT requirements from www.gov.uk.

If your driving licence is from a country in the European Union (EU), Iceland, Liechtenstein or Norway, you can drive in the UK for as long as your licence is valid.

Check that you understand:

- The fundamental principles of UK law
- That domestic violence, FGM and forced marriage are illegal in the UK
- The system of income tax and National Insurance
- The requirements for driving a car

Your role in the community

Becoming a British citizen or settling in the UK brings responsibilities but also opportunities. Everyone has the opportunity to participate in their community. This section looks at some of the responsibilities of being a citizen and gives information about how you can help to make your community a better place to live and work.

VALUES AND RESPONSIBILITIES

Although Britain is one of the world's most diverse societies, there is a set of shared values and responsibilities that everyone can agree with. These values and responsibilities include:

- to obey and respect the law
- to be aware of the rights of others and respect those rights
- to treat others with fairness
- to behave responsibly
- to help and protect your family
- to respect and preserve the environment
- to treat everyone equally, regardless of sex, race, religion, age, disability, class or sexual orientation
- to work to provide for yourself and your family
- to help others
- to vote in local and national government elections.

Taking on these values and responsibilities will make it easier for you to become a full and active citizen.

BEING A GOOD NEIGHBOUR

When you move into a new house or apartment, introduce yourself to the people who live near you. Getting to know your neighbours can help you to become part of the community and make friends. Your neighbours are also a good source of help – for example, they may be willing to feed your pets if you are away, or offer advice on local shops and services.

You can help prevent any problems and conflicts with your neighbours by respecting their privacy and limiting how much noise you make. Also try to keep your garden tidy, and only put your refuse bags and bins on the street or in communal areas if they are due to be collected.

GETTING INVOLVED IN LOCAL ACTIVITIES

Volunteering and helping your community are an important part of being a good citizen. They enable you to integrate and get to know other people. It helps to make your community a better place if residents support each other. It also helps you to fulfil your duties as a citizen, such as behaving responsibly and helping others.

How you can support your community

There are a number of positive ways in which you can support your community and be a good citizen.

JURY SERVICE

As well as getting the right to vote, people on the electoral register are randomly selected to serve on a jury. Anyone who is on the electoral register and is aged 18 to 70 can be asked to do this.

HELPING IN SCHOOLS

If you have children, there are many ways in which you can help at their schools. Parents can often help in classrooms, by supporting activities or listening to children read.

Many schools organise events to raise money for extra equipment or out-of-school activities. Activities might include book sales, toy

> **"**
> When you move into a new house or apartment, introduce yourself to the people who live near you. Getting to know your neighbours can help you to become part of the community and make friends.
> **"**

sales or bringing food to sell. You might have good ideas of your own for raising money. Sometimes events are organised by parent-teacher associations (PTAs). Volunteering to help with their events or joining the association is a way of doing something good for the school and also making new friends in your local community. You can find out about these opportunities from notices in the school or notes your children bring home.

Parents often help in classrooms, by supporting activities or listening to children read

School governors and school boards

School governors, or members of the school board in Scotland, are people from the local community who wish to make a positive contribution to children's education. They must be aged 18 or over at the date of their election or appointment. There is no upper age limit.

Governors and school boards have an important part to play in raising school standards. They have three key roles:

- setting the strategic direction of the school
- ensuring accountability
- monitoring and evaluating school performance.

You can contact your local school to ask if they need a new governor or school board member. In England, you can also apply online at the School Governors' One-Stop Shop at www.sgoss.org.uk.

In England, parents and other community groups can apply to open a free school in their local area. More information about this can be found on the Department for Education website at www.dfe.gov.uk.

SUPPORTING POLITICAL PARTIES

Political parties welcome new members. Joining one is a way to demonstrate your support for certain views and to get involved in the democratic process.

Political parties are particularly busy at election times. Members work hard to persuade people to vote for their candidates – for instance, by handing out leaflets in the street or by knocking on people's doors and asking for their support. This is called 'canvassing'. You don't have to tell a canvasser how you intend to vote if you don't want to.

British citizens can stand for office as a local councillor, a member of Parliament (or the devolved equivalents) or a member of the European Parliament. This is an opportunity to become even more involved in the political life of the UK. You may also be able to stand for office if you are an Irish citizen, an eligible Commonwealth citizen or (except for standing to be an MP) a citizen of another EU country.

You can find out more about joining a political party from the individual party websites.

HELPING WITH LOCAL SERVICES

There are opportunities to volunteer with a wide range of local service providers, including local hospitals and youth projects. Services often want to involve local people in decisions about the way in which they work. Universities, housing associations, museums and arts councils may advertise for people to serve as volunteers in their governing bodies.

You can volunteer with the police, and become a special constable or a lay (non-police) representative. You can also apply to become a magistrate. You will often find advertisements for vacancies in your local newspaper or on local radio. You can also find out more about these sorts of roles at www.gov.uk.

The Department for Education website can now be found at www.gov.uk/ government/ organisations/ department- for-education

You may also be able to stand for office if you are an Irish citizen, an eligible Commonwealth citizen or (except for standing to be an MP) a citizen of another EU country.

CHAPTER 7
Appendices

➜ IN THIS CHAPTER you will find a glossary of words and terms used throughout the chapters. You need to read through all of the listed terms and be sure that you understand all of them. Each word or phrase is fully explained in easy-to-understand language.

You will also find some useful summaries of the dates and events listed in the main chapters. These lists summarise sections of the key information but they do not give you every date or event featured in the chapters. They should be used to aid your studies and not as an alternative for studying the chapters.

IN THIS CHAPTER THERE IS:
- A glossary of key terms
- Key dates in the calendar
- A timeline of key legislation
- A timeline of key dates in how the UK is governed
- A timeline of key battles and wars

Glossary

This glossary will help readers understand the meaning of key terms which appear in the study materials. Where words may be difficult to understand, an example of their use may follow the definition.

The word that is bracketed after an entry relates to the particular context in which the word is being defined – for example, arrested (police). A slash (/) separates different definitions.

AD	Anno Domini – referring to the number of years after the birth of Jesus Christ – used as a time reference
allegiance	Loyalty to something – for example, to a leader, a faith or a country
annexed	Joined
architect	Someone who designs buildings
armed forces	The army, navy and air force which defend a country in times of peace and war
arrested (police)	Taken by the police to a police station and made to stay there to answer questions about illegal actions or activity
arson	The criminal act of deliberately setting fire to a building
assault	The criminal act of using physical force against someone or of attacking someone – for example, hitting someone
bank holiday	A day when most people have an official day off work and many businesses are closed. A bank holiday can also be called a public holiday
baron	A man who has one of the ranks of the British **nobility**. The title was particularly common during the **Middle Ages**
BC	Before Christ – referring to the number of years before Jesus Christ was born – used as a time reference
bishop	A senior member of the clergy in the Christian religion, often in charge of the churches in a particular area
boom	A sharp rise in something – very often in business activity or the economy
brutality	Behaviour towards another which is cruel and violent and causes harm

by-election	An election held in a parliamentary **constituency** or local authority area to fill a vacancy (see also **General Election**)
cabinet (government)	A group of senior ministers who are responsible for controlling government policy
casualties (medical)	People who are wounded or killed (for example, in a war)
cathedral	The most important church in an area
charter (government)	An official written statement which describes the rights and responsibilities of a state and its citizens
chieftain	The leader of a **clan** in Scotland or Ireland
civil disobedience	The refusal of members of the public to obey laws, often because they want to protest against political issues
civil law	The legal system that deals with disputes between people or groups of people
civil service	The departments within the government which manage the business of running the country – people who work for the government can be called civil servants
civil war	A war between groups who live in the same country
clan	A group of people or families who live under the rule of a **chieftain** and may be descendants of the same person – a term used traditionally in Scotland
clergy	Religious leaders, used here to describe religious leaders in Christian churches
coalition	A partnership between different political parties
colonise	Inhabit and take control of another country. People who colonise are called colonists
commemorate	Show that something or someone is remembered
composer	Someone who writes music
conquered	Beaten in battle
constituency	A specific area where the voters who live in that place (its constituents) can elect an MP to represent them in Parliament
constitution (law)	The legal structure of established laws and principles which is used to govern a country
convention (government)	An agreement, often between countries, about particular rules or codes of behaviour
criminal law	The legal system that deals with illegal activities

decree (law)	Official order, law or decision
democratic country	A country which is governed by people who are elected by the population to represent them in Parliament
devolution	The passing of power from a central government to another group at a regional or local level, which can then be called a devolved administration
dialect	A form of a language spoken by a particular group or people living in a particular area
domestic policies	Political decisions that relate to what is happening within a country (as opposed to in another country)
electoral register	The official list of all the people in a country who are allowed to vote in an election
electorate	All the people who are allowed to vote in an election
eligible	Allowed by law
ethnic origin	The country of birth, someone's race or the nationality of someone when they were born/the customs and place from which a person and their family originated (or came from)
executed	Killed as a punishment
first past the post	A system of election in which the candidate with the largest number of votes in a particular **constituency** wins a seat in Parliament
franchise	The right to vote
General Election	An event in which all the citizens of a country who are allowed to vote choose the people they wish to represent them in their government
gothic	A type of art or architecture that is based on the Middle Ages
government policies	Official ideas and beliefs that are agreed by a political party about how to govern the country
guilty	Found by a court to have done something which is illegal
heir	Someone who will legally receive a person's money or possessions after their death. The heir to the throne is the person who will become the next king or queen
House (history)	A family (for example, House of York)
household	A home and the people who live in it/something that relates to a home. (For example, household chores are tasks that are done around the house, such as cleaning and cooking)

House of Commons	That part of the **Houses of Parliament** where MPs who are elected by the voting public debate political issues
House of Lords	That part of the **Houses of Parliament** where people who have inherited their place or been chosen by the government debate political issues
Houses of Parliament	The building in London where the **House of Commons** and **House of Lords** meet
illegal	Something which the law does not allow
infrastructure	Structured network that is necessary for successful operation of a business or transport system – for example, roads or railways
innocent (law)	Found by a court not to have done something illegal
judge	The most important official in court. The judge makes sure what happens in court is fair and legal
judiciary	All the **judges** in a country. Together, they are responsible for using the law of the land in the correct way
jury (legal)	People who are chosen to sit in court, listen to information about a crime, and decide if someone is guilty or innocent
legal	Allowed to do so by law
legislative power	The power to make laws
liberty	Freedom
magistrate	A person who acts as a **judge** in a court case where the crime is not a serious one
marital status	Information about whether a person is single, married, separated or divorced. This is often asked for on official forms
media, the	All the organisations which give information to the public, i.e. newspapers, magazines, television, radio and the internet
medieval/Middle Ages	In history, the period between 1066 and about 1500
missionary	Someone who travels to teach about a religion
monarch	The king or queen of a country
national issues	Political problems that can affect everyone who lives in a country
nationalised	Bought and then controlled by central government – relating to an industry or service that was previously owned privately
nobility	The people in a country who belong to the highest social class, some of whom may have titles – for example, Lord, Duke, Baron

office, to be in	To be in power in government
Olympics	International sporting event held every four years
opposition	In the **House of Commons**, the largest political party which is not part of the government is officially known as the opposition
oratorio	A piece of music for an orchestra (musicians) and singers, often about a religious idea
Pale (history)	Part of Ireland governed by the English
party politics	The shared ideas and beliefs of an organised group of politicians
patron saint	A Christian saint who is believed to protect a particular area or group of people
penalty (law)	Punishment for breaking the law
plague	A very serious, infectious disease
Pope, the	The head of the Roman Catholic Church
portrait	A picture of a person
practise a religion	Live according to the rules and beliefs of a religion
Presbyterian	The main Protestant Church in Scotland
Prime Minister	The politician who leads the government
prohibit/ prohibition	Make something illegal
proportional representation	A system of election in which political parties are allowed a number of seats in Parliament that represents their share of the total number of votes cast
Protestants	Christians who are not members of the Roman Catholic Church
public body	A governmental department or a group of people who represent or work for the government and who work for the good of the general public
public house/ pub	A place where adults can buy and drink alcohol
Quakers	A Protestant religious group
rebellion	Organised fighting against a government
Reformation, the	The religious movement in the 16th century that challenged the authority of the **Pope** and established **Protestant** churches in Europe

refugee	A person who must leave the country where they live, often because of a war or for political reasons
residence	The place where someone lives
rival viewpoints	Opinions held by different groups of people
rural	Countryside
scrutinise	Examine all the details
seat (Parliament)	A **constituency**
sentence	A punishment imposed by a court
shadow cabinet	Senior MPs of a political party not in government
sheriff (law)	A **judge** in Scotland
slavery	A system in which people bought and sold other people (slaves) who were forced to work without pay
sonnet	A poem which is 14 lines long and rhymes in a particular way
Speaker, the	The member of the **House of Commons** who controls the way issues are debated in Parliament
stand for office	Apply to be elected – for example, as an MP or councillor
strike, to go on	Refuse to work in order to protest against something
successor (government)	A person who comes after another and takes over an office or receives some kind of power – for example, a son who becomes king when his father dies is his successor
suspend	To stop something from happening or operating, usually for a short time
terrorism	Violence used by people who want to force a government to do something. The violence is usually random and unexpected, so that no one can feel really safe from it
The Phone Book	A book which contains names, addresses and phone numbers of organisations, businesses and individuals
theft	The criminal act of stealing something from a person, building or place
trade union	An association of workers formed to protect its members
treaty	An official written agreement between countries or governments
uprising	A violent revolt or rebellion against an authority
voluntary work	Work which someone does because they want to and which they do for free, i.e. they do not receive any payment

volunteer	Someone who works for free or who offers to do something without payment (see **voluntary work**)
war effort	The work people did in order to help the country in any way they could during wartime
Yellow Pages	A book that lists names, addresses and telephone numbers of businesses, services and organisations in an area. Also available online at www.yell.com

Dates in the calendar

This page lists all the key dates of the British calendar that are mentioned in the official study materials.

1 January	New Year's Day
14 February	Valentine's Day
1 March	St David's Day
17 March	St Patrick's Day
1 April	April Fool's Day
14 April	Vaisakhi (also Baisakhi)
23 April	St George's Day
31 October	Halloween
5 November	Bonfire Night
11 November	Remembrance Day
30 November	St Andrew's Day
24 December	Christmas Eve
25 December	Christmas Day
26 December	Boxing Day
31 December	New Year's Eve / Hogmanay

Up to the Norman Conquest

This table lists the key events that happened up to and including the Norman Conquest.

Period	Monarch	Year	What?
Stone Age		6000 years ago	First farmers arrive in Britain
Roman Empire		55 BC	Julius Caesar unsuccessfully invades Britain
		AD 43	Emperor Claudius successfully invades Britain
		3rd–4th centuries	Christian communities appear in Britain
		410	The Roman army leaves Britain
Anglo-Saxon		600	Anglo-Saxon kingdoms are established in Britain
		789	The Vikings first visit Britain
Norman Conquest	William I	1066	William the Conqueror, Duke of Normandy, becomes King William I of England after defeating Harold, the Saxon King of England, at the Battle of Hastings
			Westminster Abbey first used as coronation church

The Middle Ages (1066–1485)

The Middle Ages cover the time after the Norman Conquest until the Wars of the Roses.

Century	Monarch	Year	What?
13th	John	1215	Magna Carta introduced during King John's rule
	Edward I	1284	Edward I of England introduces Statute of Rhuddlan, annexing Wales to Crown of England
14th		1314	The Scottish, led by Robert the Bruce, defeat the English at the Battle of Bannockburn
15th		By 1400	In England, official documents are written in English and English becomes the preferred language of royal court and Parliament
	Henry V	1415	The Battle of Agincourt, the most famous battle of the Hundred Years War, sees King Henry V's vastly outnumbered army beat the French
		Mid-15th century	Last Welsh rebellions are defeated. English law and language are introduced in Wales
		1450	English leave France
		1455	The Wars of the Roses start between the Houses of Lancaster and York over who should be king of England
		1485	The Wars of the Roses end with the Battle of Bosworth Field. King Richard III of the House of York is killed and Henry Tudor of the House of Lancaster becomes Henry VII

The Reformation to the Glorious Revolution

From 1485 onwards, many changes happened across Great Britain. Starting with the Reformation, there were then the Elizabethan period and the English Civil War. After the war, the Restoration happened, and the Glorious Revolution soon after that.

Period	Monarch	Year	What?
The Reformation	Henry VIII	21 Apr 1509	Henry VIII becomes king
		1530s	The Reformation in England and Wales leads to the formation of the Protestant Church
		28 Jan 1547	Henry VIII dies and Edward VI, a Protestant, becomes king
	Edward VI / Bloody Mary	1553	Edward VI dies at the age of 15, having ruled for six years. 'Bloody' Mary, a Catholic, becomes Queen
	Elizabeth I	1560	The Reformation in Scotland. The predominantly Protestant Scottish Parliament abolishes the authority of the Pope and Roman Catholic services become illegal
Elizabethan		1588	Elizabeth I defeats the Spanish Armada, which had been sent to restore Catholicism to England
		1603	Elizabeth I dies. James I of England, Wales and Ireland and VI of Scotland, Elizabeth's cousin, becomes king
English Civil War	Charles I	1640	Charles I tries to introduce a revised prayer book in Scotland, causing rebellion. He recalls Parliament to try and raise money for an army to repel the Scots. The Protestant and Puritan Parliament refuse to give Charles the money, even after the Scottish invade
		1641	Revolt begins in Ireland, where there is a Royalist army. Cromwell eventually subdues the revolt with great violence, still remembered today

Period	Monarch	Year	What?
English Civil War	Charles I	1642	Civil war begins between Royalist Cavaliers loyal to Charles I and Parliamentarian Roundheads
		1646	The Roundheads defeat Charles I's army at the Battles of Marston Moor and Naseby and take him prisoner
		1649	Charles I, who is unwilling to reach agreement with Parliament, is executed
	Cromwell	1658	Lord Protector Oliver Cromwell dies
			His son, Richard Cromwell, becomes Lord Protector
The Restoration	Charles II	1 May 1660	Charles II is invited back from exile in the Netherlands
		1679	Habeas Corpus Act becomes law
		1685	Charles II dies with no legitimate heir. His Catholic brother, James II of England, Wales and Ireland and James VII of Scotland, becomes king
The Glorious Revolution	William III	1688	William of Orange is asked to invade by important Protestants. This is the Glorious Revolution because it is non-violent. He becomes William III of England, Wales and Ireland and William II of Scotland and rules jointly with Mary, James II's elder daughter
		1689	Bill of Rights becomes law, meaning that the monarch must now be Protestant and ask Parliament for funding for the army and navy every year. Parliament now has to be elected every three years
		1690	William II/III defeats James II, brother of Charles II, at Battle of the Boyne in Ireland. James flees back to France

The 18th and 19th centuries

The 18th and 19th centuries can be referred to in many ways. The 18th century saw the Enlightenment whilst the Industrial Revolution happened in the 18th and 19th centuries. The Victorian Age lasted from 1837 until 1901. It was also during this time that the British Empire developed.

Period	Monarch	Year	What?
The Enlightenment	Anne	1707	The Act of Union 1707, known as the Treaty of Union in Scotland, creates Great Britain, the union of England, Wales and Scotland
		1714	Queen Anne dies
	George I	1714	George I (a German Protestant) becomes king
	George II	1745	Charles Edward Stuart (Bonnie Prince Charlie), grandson of James II, lands in Scotland to try and usurp George II
		1746	Bonnie Prince Charlie is defeated by George II at the Battle of Culloden. Charles escapes back to Europe
The Industrial Revolution		1776	13 American colonies declare independence, leading to the American War of Independence between the colonial and British forces
		1783	The American colonial forces defeat the British army and the independence of the colonies is recognised
		1789	Following a revolution in France, the new government declares war on Britain. Napoleon later becomes Emperor of France and continues the war
		1801	The Act of Union 1800 unifies Ireland with England, Scotland and Wales
		21 Oct 1805	The British navy, lead by Admiral Nelson, defeats the combined Spanish and French fleets at the Battle of Trafalgar. Nelson is killed in battle

Period	Monarch	Year	What?
The Industrial Revolution		1807	It becomes illegal to trade slaves in British ships or from British ports
		1815	The French Wars end with the defeat of Emperor Napoleon by the Duke of Wellington at Waterloo
		1832	The first Reform Act grants many more people the right to vote and abolishes both rotten and pocket boroughs
		1833	Emancipation Act abolishes slavery throughout the Empire. Two million Indian and Chinese workers are employed to replace the freed slaves
Victorian Age and the Industrial Revolution	Victoria	1837	Victoria becomes Queen at the age of 18
		1846	The Corn Laws are repealed, allowing the import of cheap grain
		1847	Working limits for women and children are introduced at 10 hours a day
		1853–1856	The Crimean War is fought with Turkey and France against Russia
		1867	The second Reform Act creates more urban seats in Parliament and reduces amount of property people must own in order to vote
		1870	An Act of Parliament allows women to keep their earnings, property and money when they get married

Period	Monarch	Year	What?
Victorian Age and the Industrial Revolution	Victoria	1882	An Act of Parliament gives women the right to keep their own earnings and property
		1899–1902	The Boer War is fought against Dutch settlers in South Africa. The war raises public sympathy for the Boers and leads to questioning of the Empire's role
		1901	Victoria dies after almost 64 years on the throne. At the date of writing (2013), this was the longest reign of a British monarch

The 20th century to the present day

The study materials break the 20th century down into a few sections. These are the First World War, the inter-war period, the Second World War, and then the decades that make up post-war Britain, such as the 'Swinging Sixties'.

Period	Prime Minister	Year	What?
		1913	The Home Rule Bill is introduced in Parliament proposing a self-governing Ireland with its own parliament
First World War		1914–1918	World War One (WW1)
		28 Jun 1914	Archduke Franz Ferdinand of Austria is assassinated, setting off a chain of events which leads to WWI
		1 Jul 1916	A British attack, known as the Battle of the Somme, results in 60,000 British casualties on the first day alone
		1916	Irish nationalists revolt against delays in the implementation of Home Rule for Ireland. Leaders of the failed revolt, which was known as the Easter Rising, are executed under martial law
		1918	Women over the age of 30 are given the right to vote and stand for Parliament
		11 Nov 1918	WW1 ends at 11.00 am
Inter-war period		1921	Following a guerilla war against the police and British army in Ireland, a peace treaty is signed with Irish nationalists
		1922	Ireland is separated into two countries. The six mainly Protestant counties in the north remain part of the UK as Northern Ireland. The rest of Ireland becomes the Irish Free State. A Northern Ireland Parliament is established
		1928	Women are given the right to vote at 21, the same age as men

Period	Prime Minister	Year	What?
Inter-war period		1933	Adolf Hitler comes to power in Germany
Second World War		1939	Hitler invades Poland. Britain and France declare war on Germany in response to this aggression
	Winston Churchill	1 May 1940	Winston Churchill becomes Prime Minister
		1940	German forces defeat allied troops and advance through France
		Summer 1940	The Royal Air Force wins the crucial air battle, the Battle of Britain, against the German air force
		June 1940– June 1941	Until German invasion of Soviet Union in June 1941, Britain and the Empire stand alone against Nazi Germany
		1941	The Social Insurance and Allied Services report (the Beveridge Report) is commissioned
		Dec 1941	Japan bombs US naval harbour, Pearl Harbor, and the US enters World War Two
		1942	The Social Insurance and Allied Services report (the Beveridge Report) is published by William Beveridge
		1944	R A Butler oversees introduction of the Education Act 1944 (often called 'The Butler Act') introducing free secondary education in England and Wales and creating primary and secondary stages of education
		6 Jun 1944	Allied forces land in Normandy. This is known as D-Day
		May 1945	The Allies comprehensively defeat Germany
		Aug 1945	The US drops atomic bombs on Hiroshima and Nagasaki. Japan surrenders

Period	Prime Minister	Year	What?
Post-war Britain	Clement Attlee	1945	Clement Attlee becomes Prime Minister of a Labour government after Winston Churchill loses General Election
		1947	Independence granted to nine colonies of the Empire including India, Pakistan and Ceylon (now Sri Lanka)
		1947–1967	Other colonies of the Empire in the Caribbean and Pacific achieve independence
		1948	Aneurin (Nye) Bevan, then Minister for Health, leads establishment of the NHS
		1949	Irish Free State becomes a republic
		1950	UK is one of the first countries to sign the European Convention on Human Rights and Fundamental Freedoms
	Winston Churchill	1951	Winston Churchill returns as Prime Minister after defeating Clement Attlee
		1951–64	There is a Conservative government in the UK
		1952	Elizabeth II becomes queen
		25 Mar 1957	Belgium, France, Germany, Italy, Luxembourg and the Netherlands sign the Treaty of Rome, forming the EEC
		1958	The Prime Minister is given the power to nominate life peers
'Swinging Sixties'		1960s	Strict new immigration rules require immigrants to have a connection to the UK through birth or ancestry. This leads to a fall in the numbers of immigrants coming from West Indies, India, Pakistan and what is now Bangladesh.
		1964	Winston Churchill stands down at the General Election
		1969	The voting age is reduced to 18 for men and women

Period	Prime Minister	Year	What?
1970s and The Troubles		1969	The Troubles, a conflict between those wishing for full Irish independence and those wishing to remain part of the UK, begin in Northern Ireland
		1970s	There is serious unrest in Northern Ireland, including terror campaigns
		1972	The Northern Ireland Parliament is abolished
		1973	The UK joins the EEC
Conservative government	Margaret Thatcher	1979	Margaret Thatcher, a Conservative MP, becomes Prime Minister
		1979–1990	Thatcher's Conservative government leads the UK
		1982	Argentina invades the Falkland Islands, a British overseas territory in the South Atlantic. A naval task force is sent from the UK which recovers the islands
	John Major	1990s	The UK plays a leading role in coalition forces during liberation of Kuwait following the Iraqi invasion in 1990 and the conflict in the Former Republic of Yugoslavia
Labour government	Tony Blair	1997	Tony Blair, a Labour MP, is elected as Prime Minister
		1997	Some powers are devolved from central government to give people in Wales, Scotland and Northern Ireland more control over domestic matters
		1998	The Belfast (or Good Friday) Agreement is signed in Northern Ireland, leading to the establishment of the Northern Ireland Assembly
		1998	Human Rights Act incorporates the European Convention on Human Rights and Fundamental Freedoms into UK law
		1999	The first Northern Ireland Assembly is elected

Period	Prime Minister	Year	What?
Labour government	Tony Blair	1999	The Welsh Assembly and Scottish Government are formed
		1999	Hereditary peers lose the automatic right to attend the House of Lords. They now elect a few of their number to represent them in the Lords
		Since 2000	British forces are engaged in a global fight against terrorism and the proliferation of weapons of mass destruction, including operations in Afghanistan and Iraq
		2002–2007	The Northern Ireland Assembly is suspended
	Gordon Brown	2007	Gordon Brown, a Labour MP, becomes Prime Minister
		2008	Forced Marriage Protection Orders are introduced in England, Wales and Northern Ireland, allowing the courts to issue orders to protect a person from being forced into a marriage, or a person in a forced marriage
		2009	British combat troops leave Iraq
Coalition government	David Cameron	1 May 2010	The first coalition government since Feb 1974 is elected. David Cameron, a Conservative MP, becomes Prime Minister
		2011	Forced Marriage Protection Orders are introduced in Scotland
		2011	The Welsh Assembly gets powers to pass laws on education & training, health & social services, economic development and housing
		Nov 2012	The First Police and Crime Commissioners (PCCs) are elected in England and Wales
		2012	Elizabeth II celebrates her Diamond Jubilee (60 years on the throne)
		2014	Afghanistan will have full security responsibility in all of its provinces

CHAPTER 8
Practice Tests

Preparation tips

→ **BEFORE YOU START**

The Life in the UK Test is made up of 24 multiple-choice questions. You have 45 minutes to complete the test. This means you have just under two minutes to answer each question. This is plenty of time as long as you concentrate and work steadily. However, don't spend too much time on any one question.

Before you begin the test, you can ask the test supervisor for blank paper. You will not be able to use any other materials during the test. However, you can use the supplied paper to make notes.

If you find a question difficult and are unsure of the correct answer, make a note of the question number on your blank paper. Come back to the question once you have completed the rest of the test.

Questions to expect

All questions in the Life in the UK Test are multiple-choice. There are four different formats in which a question may be asked:

1. **One correct answer** – Choose the correct answer to the question from four options

   EXAMPLE

   What important event in the development of women's rights happened in 1928?

   A Women were first given the right to vote.

   B Women were given the right to vote at the same age as men.

   C The first divorce laws were introduced.

   D Women were allowed to keep their own earnings and property.

2. **Two correct answers** – Choose two correct answers to the question from four options. You need BOTH parts to answer the question correctly.

   EXAMPLE

   Which TWO of the following are famous Paralympians?

   A Baroness Tanni Grey-Thompson

   B Dame Kelly Holmes

   C Jayne Torvill

   D Ellie Simmonds

3. **True or False** – Decide whether a statement is true or false

   EXAMPLE

   Is the statement below TRUE or FALSE?
   A newspaper's owner may try to influence government policy by running a campaign

   A True

   B False

4. **Select correct statement – Choose the correct statement from two options**

EXAMPLE

Which of these statements is correct?

A Florence Nightingale is often regarded as the founder of modern nursing.

B Florence Nightingale pioneered the use of syringes in hospitals.

WORKING THROUGH THE ANSWERS

When you start your test, make sure you read each question carefully. Make sure you understand it.

If you are confident that you know the correct answer, make your selection and move on to the next question.

It is vital that you select an answer for every question even if you are not confident that it is correct. There is a chance that even a guess will be correct! If you do this, make sure that you note the question number on your blank paper. It is possible that a question later in the test will help you to answer a question that you have found difficult.

THINGS TO WATCH OUT FOR

Some questions may be worded so that an option may be a TRUE statement but not be the CORRECT answer to the question being asked.

Be careful if questions and answers use words that are absolute. These words mean that the question or answer applies in all cases (e.g. *always*, *every*) or not at all (e.g. *never*).

EXAMPLE

Which of the following statements is correct?

A There are a few members of Parliament who do not represent any of the main political parties.

B All members of Parliament have to belong to a political party.

The second statement is absolute. There are no exceptions. This means the correct answer is A because, whether or not there are currently independent MPs in Parliament, there *can* be independent MPs in Parliament.

You also need to be careful of words that *moderate* a question or answer. When words such as *often, rarely, sometimes* and *usually* are used, this means that the question or answer is referring to something which is not always true.

EXAMPLE
Which of the following statements is correct?

A Magistrates usually don't get paid and do not need legal qualifications.

B Magistrates must be specially trained legal experts who have been solicitors for three years.

Whilst magistrates may be paid in some places, they usually work for free. Also, whilst they can have legal qualifications it is not compulsory. B is not correct in all cases, so the right answer is A.

You may get questions on dates. The study materials state you don't need to learn the dates of births and deaths, but you do have to know the dates of significant events.

EXAMPLE
When was the last successful invasion of England?

A 1066

B 1415

C 1642

D 1940

The question above relates to the Norman invasion of 1066. You do need to know the date of major events mentioned in the book.

EXAMPLE
Is the statement below TRUE or FALSE?
In the UK, people play practical jokes on each other on 1 April.

A True

B False

You need to know which festivals and celebrations happen on which date. Questions may cover the patron saints of the UK, religious festivals and public holidays.

Practice Test 1

1 **What are members of the House of Lords known as?**

- (A) MPs
- (B) Peers
- (C) Monarchs
- (D) MHLs

2 **Which of the following was signed in Northern Ireland in 1998?**

- (A) The Good Friday Agreement
- (B) The Forced Marriage (Civil Protection) Act
- (C) The European Convention on Human Rights
- (D) The Bill of Rights

3 **Which of the following statements is correct?**

- (A) The Union Flag is made up of four crosses, one for each part of the United Kingdom.
- (B) The Union Flag comprises three crosses.

4 **Is the statement below TRUE or FALSE?**
'Great Britain' refers to England, Wales, Scotland and Northern Ireland.

- (A) True
- (B) False

5 **Which of the following statements is correct?**

- (A) Mary Peters won gold at the 1976 Olympics in the 200 metres.
- (B) Mary Peters became team manager for the women's British Olympic team.

6 **The First World War ended in victory for Britain and its allies. At what exact time and date in 1918 did the war officially end?**

- (A) 11.00 am on 11 November
- (B) 10.00 am on 10 October
- (C) 6.00 am on 6 June
- (D) 8.00 am on 8 August

7 **What are these places famous for?** *Kew, Sissinghurst, Bodnant and Mount Stewart*

- (A) Castles
- (B) Gardens
- (C) Safari parks
- (D) Manor houses

8 **What religion was Elizabeth I?**

- (A) Catholic
- (B) Presbyterian
- (C) Protestant
- (D) Puritan

9 Which of these groups came to England during the Middle Ages to trade or to work?

- **A** Mercenaries from Spain
- **B** Glass manufacturers from Italy
- **C** Missionaries from Holland
- **D** Nurses from Turkey

10 Which is the largest expanse of fresh water in mainland Britain?

- **A** Lake Windermere
- **B** Loch Lomond
- **C** Derwentwater
- **D** Loch Ness

11 Who took over from Tony Blair as Prime Minister in 2007?

- **A** Ed Miliband
- **B** Alan Johnson
- **C** Gordon Brown
- **D** Alistair Darling

12 The phrase 'the Dunkirk spirit' refers to which key episode of the Second World War?

- **A** The successful evacuation of around 300,000 men from France
- **B** The invasion of Italy by Allied forces
- **C** The British attack on the Somme
- **D** The bravery of the Poles throughout the war

13 Which famous playwright and actor was born in 1564 in Stratford-upon-Avon?

- **A** Richard Arkwright
- **B** Thomas Hardy
- **C** Geoffrey Chaucer
- **D** William Shakespeare

14 Which of the following is a famous UK landmark?

- **A** The London Eye
- **B** Albert Square
- **C** The Hindoostane Coffee House
- **D** The Eisteddfod

15 What were TWO of the main occupations of Iron Age people?

- **A** Hunter-gatherers
- **B** Farmers
- **C** Craft workers
- **D** Fishermen

16 Is it legal to force someone to marry?

- **A** Yes, because children must obey their parents
- **B** No, it is never legal to force someone into marriage

17 During which period were Isambard Kingdom Brunel and Florence Nightingale alive?

- **A** Victorian
- **B** Tudor
- **C** Middle Ages
- **D** The 20th century

18 Where are minor criminal cases tried in a Justice of the Peace Court?

- **A** England
- **B** Scotland
- **C** Wales
- **D** Northern Ireland

19 Which of the following statements is correct?

- **A** The Queen is the elected leader of the Commonwealth.
- **B** The Queen is the ceremonial head of the Commonwealth.

20 The expression 'a sticky wicket' comes from which sport?

- **A** Rugby
- **B** Skating
- **C** Cricket
- **D** Golf

21 Who was Prime Minister of the Labour government elected in 1945?

- **A** Winston Churchill
- **B** Clement Attlee
- **C** William Beveridge
- **D** Tony Blair

22 What is Stormont?

- **A** The building in which the National Assembly for Wales sits
- **B** The building in which the Scottish Parliament sits
- **C** The building in which the UK Parliament sits
- **D** The building in which the Northern Ireland Assembly sits

23 Who or what is Clarice Cliff?

- **A** A famous operatic soprano
- **B** A famous landmark in Sussex
- **C** The highest point in Cornwall
- **D** A famous designer of ceramics

24 Which of the following statements is correct?

- **A** By the 18th century the slave trade was an established industry in the UK.
- **B** By the 18th century the slave trade was an established overseas industry but illegal within Britain.

Answers: Practice Test 1

1	B	Peers	p111
2	A	The Good Friday Agreement	p59
3	B	The Union Flag comprises three crosses.	p40
4	B	False	p8
5	B	Mary Peters became team manager for the women's British Olympic team.	p57
6	A	11.00 am on 11 November	p46–7
7	B	Gardens	p88–9
8	C	Protestant	p24–5
9	B	Glass manufacturers from Italy	p19–21
10	B	Loch Lomond	p95–103
11	C	Gordon Brown	p59
12	A	The successful evacuation of around 300,000 men from France	p48–51
13	D	William Shakespeare	p26
14	A	The London Eye	p95–103
15	B	Farmers	p12–3
15	C	Craft workers	p12–3
16	B	No, it is never legal to force someone into marriage	p137
17	A	Victorian	p41–3
18	B	Scotland	p130–3
19	B	The Queen is the ceremonial head of the Commonwealth.	p123–4
20	C	Cricket	p76
21	B	Clement Attlee	p52–4
22	D	The building in which the Northern Ireland Assembly sits	p115–9
23	D	A famous designer of ceramics	p85
24	B	By the 18th century the slave trade was an established overseas industry but illegal within Britain.	p37–8

Practice Test 2

1 Which of the following statements is correct?

- **A** William Caxton was the first person in England to print books using the printing press.
- **B** William Caxton wrote a collection of poems in English called The Canterbury Tales.

2 Who appoints MPs to the cabinet?

- **A** The Archbishop of Canterbury
- **B** The Queen
- **C** The Prime Minister
- **D** UK residents in the General Election

3 Why was Queen Mary given the nickname 'Bloody Mary'?

- **A** She had red hair
- **B** Because of her persecution of Protestants
- **C** She had a bad temper
- **D** Because she executed her husband

4 Which TWO of the following are famous British films?

- **A** Touching the Void
- **B** Anthem for Doomed Youth
- **C** The Third Man
- **D** The Mikado

5 Which of the following statements is correct?

- **A** St Helena and the Falkland Islands are Crown dependencies.
- **B** St Helena and the Falkland Islands are British overseas territories.

6 Is the statement below TRUE or FALSE?
Life peers are appointed by the monarch.

- **A** True
- **B** False

7 The UK belongs to which of the following?

- **A** The Women's Franchise League
- **B** The Australasian Union
- **C** The Commonwealth
- **D** The Arab League

8 Which of the following pieces of legislation gave every prisoner the right to a court hearing?

- **A** The Bill of Rights
- **B** The Habeas Corpus Act
- **C** The Statute of Rhuddlan
- **D** The Butler Act

9 Is the statement below TRUE or FALSE?
Following the abolition of slavery, two million Chinese and Indian workers were employed to replace the freed slaves.

A True

B False

10 When can citizens from the Commonwealth and other EU states vote in UK local authority elections?

A If they apply six months in advance

B After they complete the most recent census

C When they are resident in the UK

D If they are related to their MP

11 Which is the biggest stretch of water in the Lake District?

A Coniston Water

B Derwentwater

C Ullswater

D Windermere

12 Which of the following is located at Holyrood?

A The Houses of Parliament

B The National Assembly for Wales

C The Northern Ireland Assembly

D The Scottish Parliament

13 Who wrote the Harry Potter series of books?

A E L James

B R L Stevenson

C J K Rowling

D Graham Greene

14 Which of the following statements is correct?

A Henry VIII built many monasteries during his reign and was very protective of the Roman Catholic Church in England.

B Henry VIII broke with the Roman Catholic Church so he could divorce his first wife.

15 Which of these birds is traditionally associated with Christmas in the UK?

A Swan

B Swallow

C Turkey

D Penguin

16 On which day do Christians paint an ash cross on their forehead as a symbol for death and sorrow for sin?

A Ash Wednesday

B Christmas Day

C Hannukah

D Remembrance Day

17 Which of the following statements is correct?

- **A** Several Church of England bishops sit in the House of Lords.
- **B** Several Church of England bishops sit in the House of Commons.

18 What TWO effects did the Black Death have on social classes in the 14th century?

- **A** A new landowning class known as the gentry emerged
- **B** Lots of peasants survived so their wages fell
- **C** Wealthy middle classes developed in the town
- **D** Lots of Catholic priests were killed, leading to the Reformation

19 Who was victorious at the Battle of Bannockburn?

- **A** Edward I
- **B** Elizabeth I
- **C** Bonnie Prince Charlie
- **D** Robert the Bruce

20 Which part of the UK has a different voter registration system from the rest?

- **A** Scotland
- **B** Northern Ireland
- **C** Wales
- **D** England

21 Which TWO languages are spoken in the National Assembly for Wales?

- **A** Walloon
- **B** English
- **C** Welsh
- **D** Ulster Scots

22 Which of the following were music hall performers who later became television stars?

- **A** Margate and Wise
- **B** Morecambe and Wise
- **C** Maidstone and Wise
- **D** Matlock and Wise

23 Some people, particularly in Scotland, continued to support James II after his exile. What were these supporters called?

- **A** Luddites
- **B** Jacobites
- **C** Monarchists
- **D** Clans

24 Is the statement below TRUE or FALSE?
The Cenotaph in Trafalgar Square is a monument to Admiral Nelson.

- **A** True
- **B** False

Answers: Practice Test 2

1	A	William Caxton was the first person in England to print books using the printing press.	p19–21
2	C	The Prime Minister	p113
3	B	Because of her persecution of Protestants	p22–4
4	A	*Touching the Void*	p90–1
	C	*The Third Man*	
5	B	St Helena and the Falkland Islands are British overseas territories.	p8
6	A	True	p111
7	C	The Commonwealth	p123–4
8	B	The Habeas Corpus Act	p30
9	A	True	p37–8
10	C	When they are resident in the UK	p120
11	D	Windermere	p95–103
12	D	The Scottish Parliament	p122–3
13	C	J K Rowling	p86
14	B	Henry VIII broke with the Roman Catholic Church so he could divorce his first wife.	p22–4
15	C	Turkey	p69–70
16	A	Ash Wednesday	p69–70
17	A	Several Church of England bishops sit in the House of Lords.	p67
18	A	A new landowning class known as the gentry emerged	p17–8
	C	Wealthy middle classes developed in the town	
19	D	Robert the Bruce	p17
20	B	Northern Ireland	p120–1
21	B	English	p115–9
	C	Welsh	
22	B	Morecambe and Wise	p91–2
23	B	Jacobites	p31–2
24	B	False	p38–9

Practice Test 3

1   What is the name of the National Anthem of the UK?

- **A** *Land of Hope and Glory*
- **B** *I vow to thee my country*
- **C** *The Star Spangled Banner*
- **D** *God Save the Queen*

2   Who succeeded Oliver Cromwell following his death in 1658?

- **A** Charles I
- **B** Richard Cromwell
- **C** James II
- **D** Charles II

3   The Victorian period famously saw reformers leading moves to improve conditions for which section of society?

- **A** The aristocracy
- **B** The poor
- **C** The middle classes
- **D** The clergy

4   Which Scottish poet was known as The Bard?

- **A** Robert Burns
- **B** Robert the Bruce
- **C** Bonnie Prince Charlie
- **D** Robert Davidson

5   Youth Courts hear cases where the accused is what age?

- **A** Under the age of 10
- **B** Between the ages of 10 and 12
- **C** Under the age of 18
- **D** Between the ages of 10 and 17

6   Which of the following goods did the UK produce and export during the 19th century?

- **A** Spices
- **B** Tea
- **C** Cotton cloth
- **D** Tobacco

7   The Church of England is a Protestant church and has existed since which event?

- **A** The Realisation
- **B** The Reformation
- **C** The Reorganisation
- **D** The Renaissance

8   Who succeeded Margaret Thatcher as Prime Minister?

- **A** John Major
- **B** Douglas Hurd
- **C** Kenneth Baker
- **D** Norman Tebbit

9 Where in the UK is the National Horseracing Museum?

- **A** Ascot
- **B** Newmarket
- **C** Liverpool
- **D** Cheltenham

10 Is the statement below TRUE or FALSE?
Almost everyone in the UK who is in paid work has to pay National Insurance Contributions.

- **A** True
- **B** False

11 Why did Parliament look to restore Charles II to the throne?

- **A** There was no clear leader after the death of Oliver Cromwell
- **B** They shared his interest in science
- **C** They wanted a Catholic king
- **D** It was the only way to ensure peace in Scotland

12 Which of the following is a core value of the Commonwealth?

- **A** Intolerance
- **B** Slavery
- **C** Inequality
- **D** Good governance

13 Which cabinet minister is responsible for crime, policing and immigration?

- **A** Foreign Secretary
- **B** Home Secretary
- **C** Defence Secretary
- **D** Chancellor of the Exchequer

14 The House of Lords has which of the following powers?

- **A** To check laws that have been passed by the House of Lords
- **B** To hold the monarchy to account
- **C** To hire senior civil servants
- **D** To hold the government to account

15 Which of the following statements is correct?

- **A** Large numbers of Irish people emigrated to the United States after a potato famine in the 19th century.
- **B** Nearly all of the Irish people stayed in Ireland to rebuild after the potato famine in the 19th century.

16 After his death in 1965 Churchill was afforded which honour?

- **A** A state funeral
- **B** A tomb in Westminster Abbey
- **C** An annual national holiday was named after him
- **D** A burial at sea

17 Which Prime Minister oversaw the creation of the NHS?

- **A** Clement Attlee
- **B** Winston Churchill
- **C** Edward Heath
- **D** Margaret Thatcher

18 Is the statement below TRUE or FALSE?
The Royal Society is the oldest surviving scientific society in the world.

- **A** True
- **B** False

19 Who was the skating partner of Christopher Dean when they won a gold medal in the 1984 Olympic Games?

- **A** Diane Towler
- **B** Katarina Witt
- **C** Lyudmila Pakhomova
- **D** Jayne Torvill

20 During the Middle Ages, which TWO languages were used across England?

- **A** Anglo-Saxon
- **B** Welsh
- **C** Danish
- **D** Norman French

21 Is the statement below TRUE or FALSE?
Catherine of Aragon was a French princess.

- **A** True
- **B** False

22 Devolved administrations in the UK control which of the following?

- **A** Defence policy
- **B** Education
- **C** Foreign affairs
- **D** Immigration

23 Why is it good for the environment to use public transport or walk?

- **A** It burns more calories to use public transport or walk
- **B** It creates less pollution than driving a car
- **C** It leaves more space on the road for heavy goods vehicles
- **D** It is not good for the environment to use public transport or walk

24 How many children did Elizabeth I have?

- **A** 0
- **B** 1
- **C** 2
- **D** 3

Answers: Practice Test 3

1	D	*God Save the Queen*	p109
2	B	Richard Cromwell	p28–30
3	B	The poor	p41
4	A	Robert Burns	p35
5	D	Between the ages of 10 and 17	p130–3
6	C	Cotton cloth	p41–2
7	B	The Reformation	p67
8	A	John Major	p58–9
9	B	Newmarket	p77
10	A	True	p138–9
11	A	There was no clear leader after the death of Oliver Cromwell	p28–30
12	D	Good governance	p123–4
13	B	Home Secretary	p113–4
14	D	To hold the government to account	p111
15	A	Large numbers of Irish people emigrated to the United States after a potato famine in the 19th century.	p43
16	A	A state funeral	p48–52
17	A	Clement Attlee	p52–4
18	A	True	p30
19	D	Jayne Torvill	p74–5
20	A	Anglo-Saxon	p19–21
	D	Norman French	
21	B	False	p22–4
22	B	Education	p115–9
23	B	It creates less pollution than driving a car	p146
24	A	0	p27

Practice Test 4

1 Which TWO of the following bands or groups are British?

- **A** The Rolling Stones
- **B** The Jackson 5
- **C** The Beatles
- **D** The Osmonds

2 There is no place in British society for which TWO of the following?

- **A** Intolerance
- **B** Politics
- **C** Democracy
- **D** Extremism

3 Is the statement below TRUE or FALSE?
Britain and the Empire stood almost alone against Nazi Germany until the invasion of the Soviet Union in June 1941.

- **A** True
- **B** False

4 Which of the following statements is correct?

- **A** Good Friday is the day Christians commemorate the crucifixion of Jesus.
- **B** Easter Sunday is the day Christians commemorate the crucifixion of Jesus.

5 Which of the following statements is correct?

- **A** A civil servant is usually politically neutral.
- **B** A civil servant is always politically neutral.

6 Which TWO of the following are famous British artists?

- **A** Ellie Simmonds
- **B** David Allan
- **C** Francis Crick
- **D** John Petts

7 During the reigns of Henry VII and Henry VIII, English control in Ireland extended across how much of the country?

- **A** The Pale
- **B** Northern Ireland
- **C** None of it
- **D** The whole country

8 Is the statement below TRUE or FALSE?
The UK has never been a member of NATO.

- **A** True
- **B** False

9 **The Romans remained in Britain for how many years?**

   A 300

   B 400

   C 500

   D 1,000

10 **In 1690 William III defeated James II at which battle, which is still celebrated in Northern Ireland today?**

   A Battle of Bosworth Field

   B Battle of the Aughrim

   C Battle of Sligo

   D Battle of the Boyne

11 **Which of the following is associated with Christmas?**

   A Santa Claus

   B Sending anonymous cards

   C Guy Fawkes

   D Practical jokes

12 **Which composer, famously influenced by English folk music, died in 1958?**

   A Benjamin Britten

   B Henry Purcell

   C George Frederick Handel

   D Ralph Vaughan Williams

13 **What is another name used for the Church of England elsewhere in the world?**

   A Anglican Church

   B Mormon Church

   C Zen Church

   D Adventist Church

14 **Which TWO of the following work in government departments?**

   A Parliamentary Under-Secretaries of State

   B Police and Crime Commissioners

   C Police Community Support Officers

   D Secretaries of State

15 **Is the statement below TRUE or FALSE?**
It is illegal to smoke in most enclosed public spaces in the UK.

   A True

   B False

16 **Which of these countries was part of the British Empire during Victoria's reign?**

   A France

   B Switzerland

   C USA

   D India

17 **What do the words Magna Carta mean?**

- **A** Great Charter
- **B** Freedom of Speech
- **C** Bill of Rights
- **D** Great King

18 **Who wrote *Charlie and the Chocolate Factory* and *George's Marvellous Medicine*?**

- **A** Thomas Hardy
- **B** Kingsley Amis
- **C** Roald Dahl
- **D** Sir Arthur Conan Doyle

19 **On which day is it traditional to eat pancakes?**

- **A** Ash Wednesday
- **B** Shrove Tuesday
- **C** Easter Monday
- **D** Good Friday

20 **The UK signed which of the following in 1950?**

- **A** The Bill of Rights
- **B** The European Convention on Human Rights and Fundamental Freedoms
- **C** The Treaty of Rome
- **D** The Magna Carta

21 **Which town or city is famous for its celebration of the Hindu and Sikh festival of Diwali?**

- **A** Birmingham
- **B** Slough
- **C** Leicester
- **D** Plymouth

22 **Where was Charles II when he was called out of exile in May 1660?**

- **A** Spain
- **B** Scotland
- **C** France
- **D** The Netherlands

23 **Where was the first tennis club in the UK formed?**

- **A** Wimbledon
- **B** Leamington Spa
- **C** Bournemouth
- **D** Brighton

24 **Is the statement below TRUE or FALSE?**
Chief Constables are independent of government.

- **A** True
- **B** False

Answers: Practice Test 4

1	A	The Rolling Stones	p79–81
	C	The Beatles	
2	A	Intolerance	p2–3
	D	Extremism	
3	A	True	p48–52
4	A	Good Friday is the day Christians commemorate the crucifixion of Jesus.	p69–70
5	B	A civil servant is always politically neutral.	p115
6	B	David Allan	p82–3
	D	John Petts	
7	D	The whole country	p27
8	B	False	p125
9	B	400	p13
10	D	Battle of the Boyne	p31–2
11	A	Santa Claus	p69–70
12	D	Ralph Vaughan Williams	p79–81
13	A	Anglican Church	p67
14	A	Parliamentary Under–Secretaries of State	p113–4
	D	Secretaries of State	
15	A	True	p126–7
16	D	India	p41
17	A	Great Charter	p18–9
18	C	Roald Dahl	p58–9
19	B	Shrove Tuesday	p69–70
20	B	The European Convention on Human Rights and Fundamental Freedoms	p135–6
21	C	Leicester	p70–1
22	D	The Netherlands	p30
23	B	Leamington Spa	p78
24	A	True	p127–8

Practice Test 5

1 Which treaty set up the European Economic Community?

- **A** The Treaty of Lisbon
- **B** The Treaty of Geneva
- **C** The Treaty of Paris
- **D** The Treaty of Rome

2 Which of these are associated with Halloween?

- **A** Trick or treat
- **B** Fireworks
- **C** Mistletoe
- **D** Hot cross buns

3 George Frederick Handel, the German-born composer who became a British citizen, wrote which of the following?

- **A** Belshazzar's Feast
- **B** Peter Grimes
- **C** The Planets
- **D** Music for the Royal Fireworks

4 British combat troops left which country in 2009?

- **A** Syria
- **B** Afghanistan
- **C** Bosnia
- **D** Iraq

5 What were the Crusades?

- **A** A fleet of ships sent from Spain to attack England
- **B** The dissolution of the monasteries by Henry VIII
- **C** The civil war between the Royalists and the Parliamentarians
- **D** The fight for control of the Holy Land by European Christians

6 Who was Mary, Queen of Scots', son?

- **A** Duncan VI
- **B** James VI
- **C** Kenneth VI
- **D** Robert VI

7 What is Maiden Castle in Dorset an example of?

- **A** A Norman castle
- **B** A Stone Age settlement
- **C** A Roman fort
- **D** An Iron Age hill fort

8 What religion was Guy Fawkes, of Gunpowder Plot fame?

- **A** Protestant
- **B** Catholic
- **C** Methodist
- **D** Jewish

9 **Which cathedral contains a famous example of a stained glass window from the Middle Ages?**

- **A** Liverpool
- **B** Guildford
- **C** York Minster
- **D** Coventry

10 **Where must your name be recorded in order for you to vote in an election?**

- **A** Citizens' list
- **B** Civil list
- **C** Election list
- **D** Electoral register

11 **Is the statement below TRUE or FALSE?**
Following the defeat of James II at the Battle of the Boyne Irish Protestants were unable to take part in government.

- **A** True
- **B** False

12 **In 1485, the Wars of the Roses ended with which battle?**

- **A** The Battle of Bolton Field
- **B** The Battle of Bakewell Field
- **C** The Battle of Bognor Field
- **D** The Battle of Bosworth Field

13 **How is the Speaker chosen?**

- **A** The Queen appoints the Speaker
- **B** The Prime Minister appoints the Speaker
- **C** The House of Lords elects the Speaker
- **D** MPs elect the Speaker

14 **Which of the following statements is correct?**

- **A** The 1950s was a period of economic recovery and increasing prosperity for working people.
- **B** The 1950s was a period of economic decline that saw millions lose their job.

15 **Which of the following had their powers limited by the Bill of Rights in 1689?**

- **A** The Church
- **B** The Pope
- **C** Parliament
- **D** The monarch

16 **Father's Day is celebrated in which month?**

- **A** June
- **B** July
- **C** August
- **D** September

17 Which TWO of the following are responsibilities of school governors and school boards?

A To set the school's strategic direction

B To write the school curriculum

C To monitor and evaluate the school's performance

D To interview new teachers

18 Where in London is Boudicca's statue?

A Westminster Bridge

B Trafalgar Square

C Tower Bridge

D Marble Arch

19 You should notify your local police station if anyone is trying to do which TWO of the following?

A Persuade you to join a terrorist group

B Persuade you to change your beliefs

C Disagree with your beliefs

D Persuade you to join an extremist group

20 Who was king of England at the time of the Norman invasion in 1066?

A Herbert

B Hubert

C Harold

D Henry

21 Which of the following is a traditional food of Northern Ireland?

A Ulster Pasty

B Ulster Pancake

C Ulster Fishcake

D Ulster Fry

22 26 December is usually referred to as which of the following?

A Christmas Day

B New Year's Eve

C St George's Day

D Boxing Day

23 Which of the following statements is correct?

A The Anglo-Saxon king at Sutton Hoo was buried with no possessions.

B The Anglo-Saxon king at Sutton Hoo was buried inside a ship.

24 Dedham Vale on the Suffolk–Essex border is associated most with which landscape painter?

A Joseph Turner

B John Constable

C Richard Wilson

D Joshua Reynolds

Answers: Practice Test 5

1	D	The Treaty of Rome	p124–5
2	A	Trick or treat	p72–3
3	D	*Music for the Royal Fireworks*	p79–81
4	D	Iraq	p59–60
5	D	The fight for control of the Holy Land by European Christians	p17
6	B	James VI	p25
7	D	An Iron Age hill fort	p12–3
8	B	Catholic	p72–3
9	C	York Minster	p19–21
10	D	Electoral register	p120–1
11	B	False	p31–2
12	D	The Battle of Bosworth Field	p21
13	D	MPs elect the Speaker	p111–2
14	A	The 1950s was a period of economic recovery and increasing prosperity for working people.	p52–4
15	D	The monarch	p33
16	A	June	p72–3
17	A	To set the school's strategic direction	p141–3
17	C	To monitor and evaluate the school's performance	p141–3
18	A	Westminster Bridge	p13
19	A	Persuade you to join a terrorist group	p129
19	D	Persuade you to join an extremist group	p129
20	C	Harold	p15–6
21	D	Ulster Fry	p89–90
22	D	Boxing Day	p69–70
23	B	The Anglo-Saxon king at Sutton Hoo was buried inside a ship.	p13–5
24	B	John Constable	p82–3

Practice Test 6

1 Dr Sir Ludwig Guttman is generally regarded as the originator of which sporting event?

- **A** The Football World Cup
- **B** The Paralympics
- **C** The Olympic Games
- **D** The Cricket World Cup

2 Which of the following statements is correct?

- **A** Scotland was conquered by England during the Middle Ages.
- **B** Scotland remained unconquered by the English during the Middle Ages.

3 Sir Edward Elgar's *Pomp and Circumstance March No. 1* is also known as which of the following?

- **A** *Jerusalem*
- **B** The National Anthem
- **C** *Land of Hope and Glory*
- **D** *I vow to thee my country*

4 Where is the prehistoric village of Skara Brae?

- **A** The Shetland Islands
- **B** Oxfordshire
- **C** Orkney
- **D** Wiltshire

5 How did the British Empire evolve during the first half of the 20th century?

- **A** There was a mostly orderly transition to the Commonwealth
- **B** It abolished slavery after World War 1
- **C** It granted all colonies independence by 1934
- **D** It grew in size rapidly

6 The leader of the opposition appoints which of the following?

- **A** An alternative cabinet
- **B** A shadow cabinet
- **C** A judiciary cabinet
- **D** A Whig cabinet

7 Employment law concerns which of the following?

- **A** Unpaid debt
- **B** Faulty goods
- **C** Eviction
- **D** Unfair dismissal

8 What nationality is Sir Robert Watson-Watt, who developed radar in the 1930s?

- **A** Welsh
- **B** Scottish
- **C** Northern Irish
- **D** English

9   Is the statement below
    TRUE or FALSE?
    The Prime Minister is also an MP.

    A True

    B False

10 Which of the following can
    stand for public office?

    A Civil servants

    B Members of the armed forces

    C Those who are guilty of
    some criminal offences

    D British citizens born
    outside of the UK

11 Is the statement below
    TRUE or FALSE?
    *In rugby union, the Republic
    of Ireland and Northern
    Ireland form one team.*

    A True

    B False

12 Which of the following
    statements is correct?

    A In Ireland, the chieftains were
    supportive when England
    imposed Protestantism
    during the 16th century.

    B In Ireland, the chieftains fiercely
    opposed the English attempts
    to impose Protestantism
    during the 16th century.

13 Which TWO of these are
    fashion designers?

    A Alexander McQueen

    B Vivienne Westwood

    C Anthony Armstrong-Jones

    D Darcey Bussell

14 The eight-week Proms programme
    organised by the BBC is centred
    around which London venue?

    A Royal Albert Hall

    B Royal Festival Hall

    C Wembley Arena

    D Wembley Stadium

15 How often are elections for the
    European Parliament held?

    A Every three years

    B Every four years

    C Every five years

    D Every six years

16 Is the statement below
    TRUE or FALSE?
    *A Protestant Church of
    Scotland was established
    during the 16th century, and
    it became the state Church.*

    A True

    B False

17 The living conditions of slaves were very bad. In which TWO ways did some slaves respond to this?

- **A** They formed a union
- **B** Many tried to escape
- **C** Some revolted against their owners
- **D** They emigrated to places such as Russia and China

18 Which of the following became a republic in 1949?

- **A** Scotland
- **B** The UK
- **C** The Irish Free State
- **D** Cornwall

19 Which country developed the supersonic airliner, Concorde, in partnership with Britain?

- **A** France
- **B** Denmark
- **C** USA
- **D** Spain

20 How many national parks are there in England, Wales and Scotland?

- **A** 10
- **B** 15
- **C** 20
- **D** 25

21 The Scottish dish of haggis is made from which of the following?

- **A** A goat's liver
- **B** A deer's heart
- **C** A sheep's stomach
- **D** A chicken's breast

22 Young people are sent a National Insurance number before which birthday?

- **A** 13th
- **B** 15th
- **C** 16th
- **D** 18th

23 Which modern political party is still referred to sometimes as the Tories?

- **A** Liberal Democrats
- **B** Labour Party
- **C** Conservative Party
- **D** Whigs

24 Which of the following statements is correct?

- **A** The marriage between Henry VIII and Anne of Cleves ended in divorce.
- **B** The marriage between Henry VIII and Anne of Cleves ended with her execution.

Answers: Practice Test 6

1	B	The Paralympics	p74–5
2	B	Scotland remained unconquered by the English during the Middle Ages.	p17
3	C	Land of Hope and Glory	p79–81
4	C	Orkney	p12–3
5	A	There was a mostly orderly transition to the Commonwealth	p45
6	B	A shadow cabinet	p114
7	D	Unfair dismissal	p126–7
8	B	Scottish	p56–7
9	A	True	p110
10	D	British citizens born outside of the UK	p121–2
11	A	True	p77
12	B	In Ireland, the chieftains fiercely opposed the English attempts to impose Protestantism during the 16th century.	p22–4
13	A	Alexander McQueen	p85
	B	Vivienne Westwood	
14	A	Royal Albert Hall	p79–81
15	C	Every five years	p112
16	B	False	p25
17	B	Many tried to escape	p37–8
	C	Some revolted against their owners	
18	C	The Irish Free State	p47–8
19	A	France	p55
20	B	15	p94
21	C	A sheep's stomach	p89–90
22	C	16th	p138–9
23	C	Conservative Party	p33
24	A	The marriage between Henry VIII and Anne of Cleves ended in divorce.	p22–4

Practice Test 7

1 Which of the following are usually associated with Easter?

- **A** Holly
- **B** Trick or treat
- **C** Fireworks
- **D** Chocolate eggs

2 Is the statement below TRUE or FALSE?
The Bill of Rights in 1689 led to the development of party politics.

- **A** True
- **B** False

3 Which British inventor was responsible for developing the television in the 1920s?

- **A** Sir Robert Watson-Watt
- **B** Sir Bernard Lovell
- **C** John Logie Baird
- **D** John Macleod

4 Is the statement below TRUE or FALSE?
The 'King James Version' was the first English translation of the Bible.

- **A** True
- **B** False

5 Women in Britain make up approximately what proportion of the workforce?

- **A** One-half
- **B** One-quarter
- **C** One-eighth
- **D** One-third

6 Is the statement below TRUE or FALSE?
A newspaper's owner may try to influence government policy by running a campaign.

- **A** True
- **B** False

7 Which electoral system is used to elect members of the Scottish Parliament?

- **A** Proportional representation
- **B** Alternative vote
- **C** First past the post
- **D** Feudalism

8 Which of the following is paid for by National Insurance Contributions?

- **A** State retirement pensions
- **B** The armed forces
- **C** Parliamentary expenses
- **D** The Department for Work and Pensions

9   Which TWO of the following are 20th-century British discoveries or inventions?

- **A** The Turing Machine
- **B** X-Ray machines
- **C** Magnetic Resonance Imaging (MRI)
- **D** Digital calculators

10 Which TWO of these professions did Margaret Thatcher train as before becoming an MP?

- **A** Engineer
- **B** Lawyer
- **C** Chemist
- **D** Teacher

11 Is the statement below TRUE or FALSE?
The Scottish Parliament has been held in temporary accommodation since 2004, whilst its new building is under construction.

- **A** True
- **B** False

12 Which government department can issue National Insurance numbers?

- **A** The NHS
- **B** Her Majesty's Revenue and Customs
- **C** Department for Work and Pensions
- **D** Department for Communities and Local Government

13 In which English county is the Eden Project?

- **A** Cornwall
- **B** Devon
- **C** Dorset
- **D** Somerset

14 What nationality was George I?

- **A** German
- **B** Scottish
- **C** English
- **D** French

15 Who is the head of the Church of England?

- **A** The Prime Minister
- **B** The Chancellor of the Exchequer
- **C** The monarch
- **D** The Speaker

16 What is the name of the main sports stadium in Cardiff?

- **A** The Welsh Arena
- **B** The Millennium Stadium
- **C** Cardiff Park
- **D** South Wales Stadium

17 Is the statement below TRUE or FALSE?
King James II of England, Wales and Ireland was a Roman Catholic.

- **A** True
- **B** False

18 Who wrote The Planets?

- **A** Handel
- **B** Sir Edward Elgar
- **C** Gustav Holst
- **D** Benjamin Britten

**19 Is the statement below
TRUE or FALSE?**
Swansea is the capital of Wales.

- **A** True
- **B** False

**20 Whom did Henry VII marry
to form an alliance between
the House of York and the
House of Lancaster?**

- **A** Elizabeth Windsor
- **B** Elizabeth Tudor
- **C** Elizabeth of York
- **D** Elizabeth of Lancaster

**21 The Domesday Book and
the Bayeux Tapestry tell us
about England during the
time of which monarch?**

- **A** George I
- **B** Edward I
- **C** Henry VII
- **D** William I

**22 Why was there uncertainty over
the succession to the throne
during the reign of Queen Anne?**

- **A** She wanted the return
of a Catholic monarch
- **B** Scotland wanted to
choose its own king
- **C** She had no surviving heirs
- **D** Parliament refused to
recognise her heirs

23 What is the role of a civil servant?

- **A** To deliver public services
- **B** To work on tobacco plantations
- **C** To chair debates in the
House of Commons
- **D** To tell jokes and make
fun of people in court

**24 Which of the following
is a major UK city?**

- **A** Gothenburg
- **B** Madrid
- **C** Moscow
- **D** Southampton

Answers: Practice Test 7

1	D	Chocolate eggs	p69–70
2	A	True	p33
3	C	John Logie Baird	p56–7
4	B	False	p27
5	A	One-half	p65–6
6	A	True	p119
7	A	Proportional representation	p115–9
8	A	State retirement pensions	p138–9
9	A	The Turing Machine	p56–7
	C	Magnetic Resonance Imaging (MRI)	
10	B	Lawyer	p58–9
	C	Chemist	
11	B	False	p115–9
12	C	Department for Work and Pensions	p138–9
13	A	Cornwall	p95–103
14	A	German	p34
15	C	The monarch	p67
16	B	The Millennium Stadium	p74–5
17	A	True	p31
18	C	Gustav Holst	p79–81
19	B	False	p62–3
20	C	Elizabeth of York	p21
21	D	William I	p15–6
22	C	She had no surviving heirs	p34
23	A	To deliver public services	p115
24	D	Southampton	p62–3

Practice Test 8

1 Which of the following statements is correct?

A In the UK, betting and gambling were illegal until 2005.

B In the UK, betting and gambling are legal.

2 Is the statement below TRUE or FALSE?
A rebellion began in Ireland during the reign of Charles I because Catholics feared the growing power of the Puritans.

A True

B False

3 Why did a large number of Russian and Polish Jews come to Britain between 1870 and 1914?

A To look for work

B To escape persecution

C To buy cotton from British merchants

D To learn English

4 Which of the following countries is a member of the European Union?

A Turkey

B Slovenia

C Belarus

D India

5 What happens on 11 November every year?

A Bonfire Night

B Remembrance Day

C Good Friday

D Shrove Tuesday

6 Cardiff, Swansea and Newport are cities in which country of the UK?

A England

B Scotland

C Wales

D Northern Ireland

7 Which of the following is a British athlete who won gold medals at the 2004 Olympic Games?

A Sir Roger Bannister

B Dame Kelly Holmes

C Jenson Button

D Henry Purcell

8 Which war started in 1914?

A The Boer War

B The Second World War

C The First World War

D The Crimean War

9 Henry Moore became famous in which field of the arts?

- **A** As a pianist
- **B** As a theatre director
- **C** As a sculptor
- **D** As an opera singer

10 Which political party did Margaret Thatcher belong to?

- **A** Liberal Democrats
- **B** Labour
- **C** Conservative
- **D** Green

11 Which of the following statements is correct?

- **A** There were few formal limits to the king's power until 1215.
- **B** The King of England had unlimited power throughout the Middle Ages.

12 Holman Hunt, Millais and Rossetti were members of which important group of 19th-century artists?

- **A** Impressionists
- **B** Expressionists
- **C** Abstract
- **D** Pre-Raphaelites

13 The Anglo-Saxon kingdoms formed by AD 600 were:

- **A** Mainly in England
- **B** Mainly in Scotland
- **C** Mainly in Wales
- **D** Mainly in Ireland

14 Is the statement below TRUE or FALSE?
The Prime Minister appoints the cabinet.

- **A** True
- **B** False

15 Which of the following statements is correct?

- **A** Having a free press means that newspaper owners may not hold political views.
- **B** Having a free press means that newspapers are not controlled by government.

16 What were supporters of the king known as during the English Civil War?

- **A** Suffragettes
- **B** Roundheads
- **C** Cavaliers
- **D** Jesters

17 Why did George I rely increasingly on his ministers?

A He didn't understand British politics

B He wasn't interested in British politics

C He wasn't of sound mind

D He didn't speak very good English

18 Which TWO of the following are British inventions or discoveries?

A Television

B The phonograph

C The structure of DNA

D Diesel engines

19 Which of the following statements is correct?

A The British defeated Napoleon at the Battle of Waterloo, but the Duke of Wellington was killed in the fighting.

B The British defeated Napoleon at the Battle of Waterloo and the Duke of Wellington went on to become Prime Minister.

20 Is the statement below TRUE or FALSE?
Bonnie Prince Charlie won the Battle of Culloden and claimed the throne back from George II.

A True

B False

21 Which of the following is associated with Formula 1?

A Bobby Moore

B Damon Hill

C Andy Murray

D Sir Steve Redgrave

22 Where is Poets' Corner?

A St Paul's Cathedral

B Hyde Park

C Westminster Abbey

D Trafalgar Square

23 Who succeeded Charles II as king when he died in 1685?

A James II

B Henry VIII

C William III

D Anne

24 In 1918, women had to be over what age in order to vote?

A 18

B 21

C 30

D 45

Answers: Practice Test 8

1	B	In the UK, betting and gambling are legal.	p93–4
2	A	True	p28
3	B	To escape persecution	p41
4	B	Slovenia	p124–5
5	B	Remembrance Day	p72–3
6	C	Wales	p62–3
7	B	Dame Kelly Holmes	p74–5
8	C	The First World War	p46–7
9	C	As a sculptor	p82–3
10	C	Conservative	p58–9
11	A	There were few formal limits to the king's power until 1215.	p18–9
12	D	Pre-Raphaelites	p82–3
13	A	Mainly in England	p13–5
14	A	True	p113
15	B	Having a free press means that newspapers are not controlled by government.	p119
16	C	Cavaliers	p28
17	D	He didn't speak very good English	p34
18	A	Television	p56–7
	C	The structure of DNA	
19	B	The British defeated Napoleon at the Battle of Waterloo and the Duke of Wellington went on to become Prime Minister.	p38–9
20	B	False	p34–5
21	B	Damon Hill	p78
22	C	Westminster Abbey	p86–8
23	A	James II	p31
24	C	30	p106

Practice Test 9

1 Which of the following statements is correct?

- **A** Generally, Parliament supported the policies of Charles II.
- **B** Generally, Parliament opposed the policies of Charles II.

2 Which of these was a 19th-century Irish politician who favoured Home Rule for Ireland?

- **A** Robert Walpole
- **B** Ronald Reagan
- **C** Charles Stuart Parnell
- **D** David Lloyd George

3 Is the following statement TRUE or FALSE?
England has a devolved government.

- **A** True
- **B** False

4 British, Irish and eligible Commonwealth citizens can stand as candidates for which positions?

- **A** MP only
- **B** Local councillor only
- **C** MEP only
- **D** Local councillor, MP, member of a devolved assembly, or MEP.

5 Who were the Fenians?

- **A** An Irish nationalist movement
- **B** A pressure group calling for votes for women in Ireland
- **C** An Irish regiment in the British Army
- **D** A group of influential Irish academics

6 When did the Hundred Years War and the Crusades take place?

- **A** Middle Ages
- **B** During the Norman Conquest
- **C** Between 1640 and 1646
- **D** The 18th century

7 Which of the following statements is correct?

- **A** Edward VI was strongly Protestant.
- **B** Edward VI was strongly Catholic.

8 Which TWO of these books were written by Rudyard Kipling?

- **A** *Just So Stories*
- **B** *The Jungle Book*
- **C** *The Time Machine*
- **D** *Animal Farm*

9 **Which of the following is the fastest person to have sailed around the world, single-handed?**

A Dame Agatha Christie

B Dame Mary Peters

C Dame Kelly Holmes

D Dame Ellen MacArthur

10 **Is the statement below TRUE or FALSE?**
In Crown Courts, serious offences are tried in front of a judge and jury.

A True

B False

11 **Which TWO names are used for the English translation of the Bible produced during James I's reign?**

A The 'New Testament'

B The 'King James Version'

C The 'Authorised Version'

D The 'James I Version'

12 **Which of these scientists was awarded the Nobel Prize for his work with DNA?**

A Albert Einstein

B Francis Crick

C James Dyson

D Brian Cox

13 **Which of the following statements is correct?**

A In the Northern Ireland Assembly, all ministerial offices are held by the majority party.

B In the Northern Ireland Assembly, ministerial offices are shared amongst the main parties.

14 **Who suspected Mary, Queen of Scots of wanting to take the throne and kept her prisoner for 20 years?**

A Elizabeth I

B Henry VIII

C Edward VI

D Charles I

15 **Which of the following statements is correct?**

A Sir Isaac Newton was a famous scientist.

B Sir Isaac Newton was a famous composer.

16 **How long is a driving licence from a country outside the EU, Norway, Liechtenstein or Iceland valid for in the UK?**

A 2 months

B 6 months

C 12 months

D 24 months

17 Is the statement below TRUE or FALSE?
There are a total of five notes in UK currency – £5, £10, £20, £50 and £100.

- **A** True
- **B** False

18 By the 1760s there were substantial British colonies in which part of the world?

- **A** North America
- **B** South America
- **C** Russia
- **D** The Middle East

19 The Anglo-Saxon kingdoms in England united under which king to defeat the Vikings?

- **A** Cnut
- **B** Ethelred the Unready
- **C** Edgar I
- **D** Alfred the Great

20 Which of the following does a new citizen swear in an oath to the Queen?

- **A** To be faithful to the Queen and her heirs
- **B** To vote the way the Queen instructs
- **C** To place a portrait of the Queen in his or her house
- **D** To worship the Queen

21 Is the statement below TRUE or FALSE?
England has never had a Danish king.

- **A** True
- **B** False

22 What does every person in the UK receive, by law?

- **A** Different treatment, depending on how wealthy he or she is
- **B** Different treatment, depending on his or her job
- **C** Equal treatment
- **D** Different treatment, depending on whether the person is male or female

23 Is the statement below TRUE or FALSE?
Queen Elizabeth II celebrated her Platinum Jubilee in 2012.

- **A** True
- **B** False

24 Who was the 17th-century organist who developed a particularly British style of church and opera music?

- **A** John Rutter
- **B** Henry Purcell
- **C** Sir Edward Elgar
- **D** Benjamin Britten

Answers: Practice Test 9

1	A	Generally, Parliament supported the policies of Charles II.	p30
2	C	Charles Stuart Parnell	p43
3	B	False	p107
4	D	Local councillor, MP, member of a devolved assembly, or MEP	p143
5	A	An Irish nationalist movement	p43
6	A	Middle Ages	p17
7	A	Edward VI was strongly Protestant.	p22–4
8	A	*Just So Stories*	p45
	B	*The Jungle Book*	
9	D	Dame Ellen MacArthur	p74–5
10	A	True	p130–3
11	B	The 'King James Version'	p27
	C	The 'Authorised Version'	
12	B	Francis Crick	p56–7
13	B	In the Northern Ireland Assembly, ministerial offices are shared amongst the main parties.	p115–9
14	A	Elizabeth I	p25
15	A	Sir Isaac Newton was a famous scientist.	p31
16	C	12 months	p139
17	B	False	p64
18	A	North America	p38
19	D	Alfred the Great	p15
20	A	To be faithful to the Queen and her heirs	p109
21	B	False	p15
22	C	Equal treatment	p126–7
23	B	False	p107–9
24	B	Henry Purcell	p79–81

Practice Test 10

1 Is the statement below TRUE or FALSE?
The European Union was previously called the European Economic Community.

- **A** True
- **B** False

2 The longest distance in mainland Britain, at 870 miles (1,400 kilometres), is between John O'Groats and where?

- **A** Land's End
- **B** Dover
- **C** Bournemouth
- **D** Bideford

3 Are local authorities elected bodies?

- **A** Yes, except in rural areas, where they are appointed by local business owners
- **B** Yes, local authorities are always elected

4 Who designed the Queen's House at Greenwich?

- **A** Sir Christopher Wren
- **B** Inigo Jones
- **C** Sir John Vanbrugh
- **D** Richard Cassels

5 Where was William Shakespeare born?

- **A** Stratford
- **B** Stratford-upon-Avon
- **C** Bradford-on-Avon
- **D** Bradford

6 Which battle of the Hundred Years War took place in 1415?

- **A** Battle of Bannockburn
- **B** Battle of Cravant
- **C** Battle of Agincourt
- **D** Battle of Hastings

7 Which of the following statements is correct?

- **A** The BBC is financed by selling space for adverts during television shows.
- **B** Funds from TV licences finance the BBC.

8 What did the Roman army do in AD 410?

- **A** Invade Ireland
- **B** Leave Britain
- **C** Invade Scotland
- **D** Defeat Boudicca

9 **Is the statement below TRUE or FALSE?**
Norwich and Bristol are cities in Wales.

- **A** True
- **B** False

10 **Is the statement below TRUE or FALSE?**
Charles II organised settlements known as plantations across Ireland.

- **A** True
- **B** False

11 **Which of the following statements is correct?**

- **A** It is only possible to register as a blood donor by visiting your local hospital.
- **B** It is possible to register as a blood donor online.

12 **Who or what were jesters?**

- **A** Silver coins of the 18th century
- **B** Combatants on horseback at medieval feasts
- **C** People who told jokes at medieval royal courts
- **D** Men who organised hunts in the Middle Ages

13 **The four shortlisted works for the Turner Prize are shown at which London venue?**

- **A** British Museum
- **B** Tate Britain
- **C** National Gallery
- **D** Victoria and Albert Museum

14 **Is the statement below TRUE or FALSE?**
Protestantism developed as a result of the Reformation.

- **A** True
- **B** False

15 **The Brit Awards is an annual event that gives awards in which industry?**

- **A** Television
- **B** Sport
- **C** Music
- **D** Film

16 **Which of the following is a Jewish festival celebrating the Jews' struggle for religious freedom?**

- **A** Vaisakhi
- **B** Eid al-Fitr
- **C** Hannukah
- **D** Diwali

17 Who was the first person to sail single-handed round the world?

- **A** Sir Francis Drake
- **B** Sir Francis Walsingham
- **C** Sir Francis Chichester
- **D** Sir Robin Knox-Johnston

18 Who was Geoffrey Chaucer?

- **A** Author of *The Canterbury Tales*
- **B** Archbishop of Canterbury
- **C** Lord Protector
- **D** Leader of the House of Commons

19 Where is Stormont located?

- **A** Belfast
- **B** Cardiff
- **C** London
- **D** Edinburgh

20 Is the statement below TRUE or FALSE?
A responsibility of Police and Crime Commissioners is to set local policing budgets.

- **A** True
- **B** False

21 In 2007, television viewers voted which of these as 'Britain's Favourite View'?

- **A** Wastwater
- **B** Buttermere
- **C** Grasmere
- **D** Bassenthwaite Lake

22 Is the statement below TRUE or FALSE?
In the Iron Age, people spoke Latin in Britain.

- **A** True
- **B** False

23 Housing, debt, employment and consumer rights are covered by which law?

- **A** Civil law
- **B** Criminal law
- **C** Military law
- **D** No laws

24 If a member of Parliament (MP) resigns or dies, what is the election that is held to replace them called?

- **A** Re-election
- **B** General Election
- **C** By-election
- **D** Fresh election

Answers: Practice Test 10

1	A	True	p124–5
2	A	Land's End	p62
3	B	Yes, local authorities are always elected	p115
4	B	Inigo Jones	p84–5
5	B	Stratford-upon-Avon	p25–6
6	C	Battle of Agincourt	p17
7	B	Funds from TV licences finance the BBC.	p92–3
8	B	Leave Britain	p13–5
9	B	False	p62–3
10	B	False	p27
11	B	It is possible to register as a blood donor online.	p144
12	C	People who told jokes at medieval royal courts	p91–2
13	B	Tate Britain	p82–3
14	A	True	p22–4
15	C	Music	p79–81
16	C	Hannukah	p70–1
17	C	Sir Francis Chichester	p78
18	A	Author of *The Canterbury Tales*	p19–21
19	A	Belfast	p122–3
20	A	True	p127–8
21	A	Wastwater	p95–103
22	B	False	p12–3
23	A	Civil law	p126–7
24	C	By-election	p112

Practice Test 11

1 PCSOs support police by doing which TWO of the following?

- **A** Independently investigating crime
- **B** Patrolling the streets
- **C** Helping the police at crime scenes
- **D** Trying suspected criminals in court

2 Ted Hughes and John Masefield are both famous as what?

- **A** Poets
- **B** Novelists
- **C** Painters
- **D** Sculptors

3 Where is the land formation of the Giant's Causeway?

- **A** Northern Ireland
- **B** Scotland
- **C** England
- **D** Wales

4 Which of the following statements is correct?

- **A** Elizabeth I was a popular monarch, particularly after the English defeat of the Spanish Armada.
- **B** Elizabeth I was an unpopular monarch because she caused religious instability.

5 On St David's Day in Wales, which flower would you expect to see people wearing?

- **A** Daffodil
- **B** Primrose
- **C** Gladioli
- **D** Aster

6 Which crop failed in Ireland in the mid-19th century, leading to a devastating famine?

- **A** Cabbages
- **B** Wheat
- **C** Potatoes
- **D** Sweetcorn

7 People can be randomly chosen for jury service if they are which TWO of the following?

- **A** A member of the police
- **B** On the electoral register
- **C** Aged at least 50
- **D** Aged between 18 and 70

8 Which devolved government has been suspended several times?

- **A** The National Assembly for Wales
- **B** The Northern Ireland Assembly
- **C** The Scottish Parliament
- **D** The UK Parliament

9   **Which of the following statements is correct?**

A   The Axis powers in the Second World War were Germany, Italy and Japan.

B   The Axis powers in the Second World War were Germany, Russia and China.

10 **Near which of these cities is Europe's longest dry ski slope?**

A   London

B   Leeds

C   Belfast

D   Edinburgh

11 **Which of the following statements is correct?**

A   If a public body does not respect an individual's rights, the judiciary will change human rights legislation.

B   If a public body does not respect an individual's rights, the judiciary can order it to change its policies or pay compensation (or both).

12 **Gertrude Jekyll is famous for her designs in which field?**

A   Fashion

B   Gardening

C   Silverware

D   Pottery

13 **What information will staff at polling stations ask from voters?**

A   Who they are voting for

B   How many votes they wish to cast

C   Who their relatives are

D   Their name and address

14 **Where did the Vikings form their first communities in Britain?**

A   Wales and Scotland

B   Eastern England and Scotland

C   Northern Ireland and Wales

D   South-west England and Wales

15 **May anyone look at the electoral register?**

A   No, only government officials can look at the register

B   Yes, but only under supervision

16 **Which of the following statements is correct?**

A   The Crimean War was the first war to receive extensive media coverage through photographs and news stories.

B   The Boer War was the first war to receive extensive media coverage through photographs and news stories.

17 **In which month do most local authorities hold elections?**

- **A** January
- **B** March
- **C** May
- **D** September

18 **In 1805, Britain's navy fought combined fleets from which nations to win the Battle of Trafalgar?**

- **A** France and Spain
- **B** Spain and Italy
- **C** France and Italy
- **D** France and the Netherlands

19 **A driving licence from which of these countries is equal to a full UK driving licence?**

- **A** USA
- **B** Norway
- **C** Australia
- **D** Canada

20 **Who was Samuel Pepys?**

- **A** A 17th-century architect
- **B** A 17th-century diarist
- **C** A 17th-century playwright
- **D** A 17th-century clergyman

21 **Which of the following statements is correct?**

- **A** To get a UK driving licence you must pass a driving test of both your knowledge and practical skills.
- **B** To get a UK driving licence you must own a car and pass a driving test of both your knowledge and practical skills.

22 **Is the statement below TRUE or FALSE?**
All solicitors are trained lawyers, but each one specialises in a particular area of law.

- **A** True
- **B** False

23 **Which of the following great thinkers or scientists is associated with the Enlightenment?**

- **A** Edwin Lutyens
- **B** Keith Campbell
- **C** Roald Dahl
- **D** James Watt

24 **Which TWO of the following were eminent film directors?**

- **A** Sir Alexander Korda
- **B** Sir Alex Ferguson
- **C** Sir Alfred Hitchcock
- **D** Sir Alexander Fleming

Answers: Practice Test 11

1	**B**	Patrolling the streets	p127–8
	C	Helping the police at crime scenes	
2	**A**	Poets	p86–8
3	**A**	Northern Ireland	p95–103
4	**A**	Elizabeth I was a popular monarch, particularly after the English defeat of the Spanish Armada.	p24–5
5	**A**	Daffodil	p88–9
6	**C**	Potatoes	p43
7	**B**	On the electoral register	p141
	D	Aged between 18 and 70	
8	**B**	The Northern Ireland Assembly	p115–9
9	**A**	The Axis powers in the Second World War were Germany, Italy and Japan.	p48–52
10	**D**	Edinburgh	p78
11	**B**	If a public body does not respect an individual's rights, the judiciary can order it to change its policies or pay compensation (or both).	p129–30
12	**B**	Gardening	p84–5
13	**D**	Their name and address	p121
14	**B**	Eastern England and Scotland	p15
15	**B**	Yes, but only under supervision	p120–1
16	**A**	The Crimean War was the first war to receive extensive media coverage through photographs and news stories.	p42–3
17	**C**	May	p115
18	**A**	France and Spain	p38–9
19	**B**	Norway	p139
20	**B**	A 17th-century diarist	p30
21	**A**	To get a UK driving licence you must pass a driving test of both your knowledge and practical skills.	p139
22	**A**	True	p134–5
23	**D**	James Watt	p35
24	**A**	Sir Alexander Korda	p90–1
	C	Sir Alfred Hitchcock	

Practice Test 12

1 Charlie Chaplin (or Sir Charles Chaplin) became famous in which type of film?

- **A** Cowboy
- **B** Cartoon
- **C** Romance
- **D** Silent

2 Which of these characters appear in books by Charles Dickens?

- **A** Harry Potter
- **B** Dr Jekyll
- **C** Lucky Jim
- **D** Mr Micawber

3 Is the statement below TRUE or FALSE?
A living person may never donate an organ.

- **A** True
- **B** False

4 Which of the following happened in 1707?

- **A** Scotland signed the Act of Union, creating the Kingdom of Great Britain
- **B** The Hundred Years War began
- **C** The English Civil War Ended
- **D** The Emancipation Act abolished slavery

5 Is the statement below TRUE or FALSE?
Richard Arkwright is particularly remembered for his wig-making.

- **A** True
- **B** False

6 Which of the following statements is correct?

- **A** St Augustine and St Columba were early Christian missionaries.
- **B** St Augustine and St Columba were leaders who fought against the Romans.

7 Which South American country invaded the Falkland Islands in 1982?

- **A** Peru
- **B** Argentina
- **C** Chile
- **D** Bolivia

8 The Muslim prophet Ibrahim was willing to sacrifice which of his family to God?

- **A** His wife
- **B** His daughter
- **C** His mother
- **D** His son

9 Which TWO of the following are public holidays in the UK?

A Mother's Day

B Easter Monday

C Good Friday

D New Year's Eve

10 What is *Auld Lang Syne*?

A The Scottish name for Edinburgh Castle

B A song written by Robert Burns, traditionally sung at New Year

C A Shakespeare play written about a Scottish king

D The Scottish name for New Year's Eve

11 What was Sir Christopher Cockerell famous for developing in the 1950s?

A The hovercraft

B The submarine

C The robot

D The glider

12 Which of the following statements is correct?

A Parliament refused to give Charles I money because they did not agree with his religious and foreign policies.

B Parliament refused to give Charles I money because they did not want to anger the bishops.

13 Which of the following statements is correct?

A James VI of Scotland was Catholic, like his mother Mary.

B James VI of Scotland was Protestant.

14 Lord Olivier gave his name to which auspicious theatre awards?

A The Lord Olivier Oscars

B The Olivier Globes

C The Laurence Olivier Awards

D The Olivier Theatrical Medals

15 What did the Welsh government need until 2011?

A To hold its sessions in Westminster

B Its First Minister to be appointed by the Prime Minister

C Approval from the UK Parliament for all laws passed

D To share ministerial offices between the main parties

16 What is one of the ways in which parents can help in schools?

A They can teach classes

B They can replace the head teacher

C They can do the children's homework for them

D They can listen to children read in the classroom

17 What is Emmeline Pankhurst associated with?

A Establishing the first training school for nurses

B Discovering penicillin in 1928

C Successfully protesting for voting age and gender equality

D Becoming the first woman Prime Minister of the UK

18 Which TWO of these film franchises are British?

A Harry Potter

B Indiana Jones

C Batman

D James Bond

19 Which of the following plays, opening in 1952 in London, has achieved the longest initial run of any show in history?

A Cats

B The Mousetrap

C HMS Pinafore

D Romeo and Juliet

20 Which of the following statements is correct?

A The Scottish Parliament was formed in 1999.

B The Scottish Parliament was formed in 2001.

21 Which is the most well-known rugby league competition for clubs?

A Super League

B Premier League

C Championship League

D Elite league

22 Which party, led by Winston Churchill, was in government between 1951 and 1964?

A Conservative

B Labour

C Liberal Democrats

D Green

23 Is the statement below TRUE or FALSE?
Military training for young people is provided by the National Citizen Service.

A True

B False

24 Which country makes up most of the total UK population?

A England

B Northern Ireland

C Scotland

D Wales

Answers: Practice Test 12

1	D	Silent	p90–1
2	D	Mr Micawber	p85–6
3	B	False	p144
4	A	Scotland signed the Act of Union, creating the Kingdom of Great Britain	p34
5	B	False	p35–7
6	A	St Augustine and St Columba were early Christian missionaries.	p13–5
7	B	Argentina	p58–9
8	D	His son	p70–1
9	B	Easter Monday	p69–73
	C	Good Friday	
10	B	A song written by Robert Burns, traditionally sung at New Year	p34–5
11	A	The hovercraft	p56–7
12	A	Parliament refused to give Charles I money because they did not agree with his religious and foreign policies.	p27–8
13	B	James VI of Scotland was Protestant.	p25
14	C	The Laurence Olivier Awards	p81–2
15	C	Approval from the UK Parliament for all laws passed	p115–9
16	D	They can listen to children read in the classroom	p141–3
17	C	Successfully protesting for voting age and gender equality	p43–4
18	A	Harry Potter	p90–1
	D	James Bond	
19	B	*The Mousetrap*	p81–2
20	A	The Scottish Parliament was formed in 1999.	p115–9
21	A	Super League	p77
22	A	Conservative	p52–4
23	B	False	p144–6
24	A	England	p64–5

WELL
DONE!

You've just read the complete
testable materials and
taken 12 full tests.

Best of luck for your official
Life in the UK Test.

Let us know how it goes at
www.lifeintheuk.net/feedback.

We'd love to hear your
experiences, good or bad, or any
suggestions you have to help us
make our products better.

Get the BritTest app

Take practice tests wherever you go with hundreds of questions and randomised practice tests in your hand.

The essential revision aid for anyone on the move. Find out more at **www.lifeintheuk.net/app.**